The Agony of the Leaves

ILLUSTRATED BY
MARK GAGNON

Helen Gustafson

Preface by
Samuel H. G. Twining, O.B.E.

Henry Holt and Company
New York

The Agony of the Leaves

THE ECSTASY OF MY LIFE WITH TEA

Henry Holt and Company, Inc.
Publishers since 1866
115 West 18th Street
New York, New York 10011

Henry Holt ® is a registered trademark of Henry Holt and Company, Inc.

Library of Congress Cataloging-in-Publication Data
Gustafson, Helen.
The agony of the leaves: the ecstasy of my life with tea / Helen Gustafson. —1st Henry Holt ed.
p.   cm.
1. Tea.   2. Cookery.   3. Gustafson, Helen—Anecdotes.   I. Title.
TX817. T3G87   1996   96-1706
641.3′372—dc20   CIP

ISBN 0-8050-3845-0

Henry Holt books are available for special promotions and premiums.
For details contact: Director, Special Markets.

First Edition—1996

DESIGNED BY KATE NICHOLS
ILLUSTRATIONS BY MARK GAGNON

Printed in the United States of America
All first editions are printed on acid-free paper.∞
1   3   5   7   9   10   6   4   2

For
Sabina Thorne Johnson,
who first saw my life
in tea

CONTENTS

PREFACE

by Samuel H. G. *Twining,* O.B.E.

This little book is the charming story of a life entwined with tea. Helen Gustafson takes us on a journey that reawakens a gentle, civilized sense of values which is often lost to most of us in the pace of modern life.

Her obvious pleasure in the adventures of everyday life is woven through a good deal of practical tea information and history that is very much needed. The title, for instance, comes from an old tea taster's expression for the dramatic moment when tea leaves unfold "as boiling water is applied"—so wrote William Ukers, author of the famous bible of tea, *All About Tea,* which first appeared in 1935.

With *The Agony of the Leaves,* Helen Gustafson makes a warm and inviting addition to that world of tea literature once inhabited by Ukers, and it is my hope that you will chuckle and sip your way through the book, just as I did.

ACKNOWLEDGMENTS

A story buried in a promotional tea pamphlet published in 1884 tells of a Mr. Pumphrey, the headmaster of one of those overdignified rural "academies" so popular in the early 1800s. He was sent abroad by his small staff to "recruit his health." That warm gesture, with its inherent sense of confidence, caught my eye. I imagine Mr. Pumphrey as slight, with a small bald spot, and awfully earnest. His health sounded not far away, needing only to be found and retrieved.

When he returned, flourishing, the headmaster found his school to be flourishing as well. In a burst of gratitude he mounted a grand tea party for staff and students and, eventually, most of the village. He hired the town hall and contrived to have it whitewashed. The students fell to, everyone pitching in to scrub the floors, pin up swags of flowers, and ready bonfires under cauldrons needed to brew the quantities of tea. Competition ran high among the volunteers as to who would be "runners," bearing the steaming pots to "dampened and smoothed" white tablecloths set with precise rows of sandwiches and tea cakes. Think of the suspense. For many of the 150 souls who attended, this was the first tea party of their lives.

Inspired by Mr. Pumphrey's example, I gave all those who helped me recruit my memories and the tea lore for this little book a grand party of their own. On the day, an hour before the official first moment, Mary Goldstein was there with English cheer and advice, as she had been when chapter two was the draft of a short story. At 3:00 P.M. sharp, the sun sparkled on the first pots of Darjeeling from the classic Castleton gardens. The doorbell rang, and the first guests arrived, the major players from San Francisco—Norwood Pratt, Roy and Grace Fong, David Hoffman, and, in a spiffy checkered jacket and exuding businesslike charm, the principal tea broker for the West Coast, Mike Spillane. They ate sparingly but dug into the tea, recupping themselves often.

Next came Jackie Mallorca, trim as usual in a smart suit and hat. She aproned herself, then helped cut and arrange the nut breads and Motorloaf (chapter five), nestling among them one of her special wheat-free breads. All was in proper order when the Chez Panisse gang began to appear. First was Alice Waters, in a characteristic black cloche and carrying an armload of early-summer flowers, which she set out in vases around the house and on the deck. Alan Tangren, forager for the restaurant and stand-in as tea chieftain when I was deep in writing or revising, brought a basket of special clementines.

Lindsey and Charles Shere were close behind, accompanied by Lindsey's sister, Pat Edwards. Each of them carried a toaster, for Pepper Toast (chapter seven). It was Lindsey and Charles who had recalled that the original recipe was in a loose-leaf file kept by David Goines, and Pat, my "librarian," had found both the file and the recipe itself. The trio sped off to plug in toasters and make the toasts, the perfect party starters.

With everything well under way, I phoned old friends and neighbors in Minnesota—Ann (Mrs. Robert) Worcester, an endless fountain of information on the Faculty Women's Club, and Ardis (Mrs. A. O. C.) Nier, date-bar source and finder of long-forgotten names. The three of us had a good chew on a conference call.

The doorbell rang again, and in stepped Mary Dadd, wearing a prim skirt and blouse much like the one she wore to the "Big Backyard Tea-in" (chapter four) some twenty years ago. She wound her way to the trifle, which she tasted and pronounced "still the best ever." Following her through the door and back to the kitchen were Dorothy Calimeris and Narsai David. As I began work on the book, both had offered generous and articulate advice, which made their arriving together a pleasant coincidence. Dorothy, in another nod to the Tea-in, unveiled her jam cake, then progressed to the backyard to reenact her role as Dispensing Angel. A knot of eager guests trailed after her from deck to yard, everyone carrying food, drink, and conversation into the sun.

A burst of activity and excited voices at the front door brought me back in to see who and what. Mitzi McClosky had arrived, and a crowd gathered as if for a celebrated aunt who invariably brings long-awaited gifts. The nephews and nieces bobbed up and down with praise and thanks for her aid as therapist and career counselor. Her guidance around important corners had helped many there, including me. With cups of Champagne, and the Champagne of teas (Darjeeling), all toasted this petite and smiling muse.

As that group moved into the living room, another group climbed the steps—the crew from the copy center: Mehrdad Goosheh, Maricela Lara, and Sandhya Frantz. Right behind them came Big Brian Preston, the express-delivery driver who, like the rest, was always ready with an encouraging word. Boyard Rowe, another copy-service super-ally, calm as always, reached for his cuppa and grinned contentedly.

The phone rang throughout the afternoon with calls from the transcontinentally challenged. The Four Corner ladies from South Dakota (chapter eight)—Wilma and Bulah and Bertha—checked in, all about to start supper. We then called "in town" to Nelson Drug to thank Julie Seas and to ask her to relay messages to Ann Halverson next door and Lori Bjorklund down the street. All three had helped with faxes and express packages and photos that were taken on hot, windy days.

No sooner had I hung up than the phone rang again, this time with a call from New York. Ray Roberts, who must be the most patient and gracious editor on the East Coast, asked if "the folks out there can handle all that agony." All toasted him. A minute later Helen Pratt rang up on her way out to dinner. An angel of an agent, she had fostered in me that spirit of "the little engine that could" all the way from idea to final page. Another delicious toast. On impulse I called Ben Ratliff at Holt and thanked him for his serenity, deftness, and dispatch.

I thought about calling Sam Twining, who had generously read the manuscript. But Judy Coburn, another careful reader, reminded me that London time was 1:00 A.M. and urged that we let the dear man sleep through the party. Rutabaga Ruth, who hates big gatherings, had called the day before. She allayed my anxieties over the party just as she had over so many things since we met at age two.

As if bridging the old days and the new among academics, Darrell Corti came though the door dressed, as usual, in Milanese elegance. He joined the tea experts for a serious discussion of protocol for the evaluating of green teas.

Moving from group to group, making sure that everyone and everything would be attended to, was phrase-meister Fritz Streiff. I had employed his wizardry to avoid pitfalls and find smooth paths for my sometimes impetuous prose. Helping him to keep the flow going that day, as they had during the days of writing, were quiet savant Steve Siegelman and C. H. (Gus) Gustafson, my helpmate for longer than I dare think about. All three were making sure that pots and cups were replenished and that cakes, trifle, and toasts remained within easy reach.

By special dispensation of the tea gods, the late-afternoon fog remained outside the Golden Gate, giving the last stages of the party a balmy air. By ones and twos the guests found me to deliver thanks and say their good-byes. As if by way of benediction, two more calls came in—one from Dr. Ronald Berman, my allopathic physician, and the other from Dr. Miki Shima, my acupuncturist and diagnostic expert. I often describe Dr. Shima as the man who, after five years, handed my health back to me as gracefully as cake on a plate of china. My renewed energy was apparent as I started to clean up immediately. But Gus insisted that we sit down and enjoy the glorious mess—and savor the party.

Mother and Muttie weren't there—but of course they were, hovering around the sun room plates. The yellow one, with its pale red flower, held the shards of Motorloaf, and my favorite, the orange cookie plate, was now invitingly strewn with scattered seedcake crumbs. I knew Mother and Muttie would be nodding and smiling to see that I had, surprisingly, learned one lesson without being told: the essentials of a full life can begin with a good pot of tea.

The Agony of the Leaves

Chapter One

TEATIME IN THE SUN ROOM

When I was a child and the world seemed as sunny and secure as my family's big red brick house on the hill, we had tea every day except Sundays. Teatime remains fixed in my memory as a time of great happiness, since it was the hour when discipline was suspended, all admonishments were silenced, and I became, so to speak, a member of the wedding, a full-fledged person of the household.

We always had tea in the sun room—an airy perch overlooking the sloping lawn above a well-trafficked corner of our genteel neighborhood in Saint Paul, Minnesota. It was a room stuffed with good things. The sun poured through what seemed like hundreds of tiny windowpanes, drenching the piano, my Austrian grandmother Muttie's chocolate brown overstuffed chair, the creaky rocker left over from her parsonage days, pots and pots of ivy, hyacinths, paper-whites, cacti, espaliered vines of all kinds, books and papers, baskets of knitting, the Chinese checkers set, my tiny red-robed Chinese doll—all these lovely things crammed in a room set against a dazzling green-plaid linoleum floor.

The friendly-looking house was set high on a ridge overlooking the flats of

Minneapolis and surrounded by sheltering elms and oaks. It had been built in 1931 by carpenters who needed work and who therefore added every possible extra that could be dreamt of. The construction was tighter than code, the paneling was hand-carved, the cupboards and under-the-stairs closets and cubbyholes were numerous and perfect for hide-and-seek. There were laundry chutes and maids' buttons (although there were never maids). The moment you stepped into the house you felt like you were in a serene and benign stronghold.

The wood paneling was warm and the conveniences lavish, but the furnishings were almost excruciatingly plain. The oak floors were bare except for two dull-colored "Persian" rugs purchased at Montgomery Ward, as were the color lithographs of sylvan scenes—perfect partners for the simple Mission-style furniture my grandfather Papa had made, and for the collection of hand-me-downs from Methodist parsonage life. Even though the house often seemed silent and dour, it was solid and safe, and I sensed correctly that we were privileged. Our income, though small, was secure; we were an academic family, and faculty salaries were protected during the Depression. I felt a little bit like a princess living on top of the hill in her pretty red castle.

My father, whom we always called Daddy, was the chairman of the Physics Department at the University of Minnesota. Under his aegis the second atom smasher ever was built, leading to discoveries that ushered in the atomic age. Suddenly, not long after World War II began, physicists from his department started leaving, which meant a series of farewell dinner parties. Professor Oppenheimer's departure was a big loss to the department, of course—but not to Mother. He was an on-again-off-again vegetarian who could arrive at a stuffed–pork chop dinner and announce imperiously, "I'll have an egg!" Mother was always caught off guard. The cream of Physics was off to work on the Manhattan Project. I thought they were all going to New York!

Even in the early gut-wrenching days of the war, I could count on teatime; the door to the sun room would be open, and light would spill into the long dark back hall. The sound of gentle conversation beckoned over the soft click-click of knitting needles, a perfect background for gossip. Not scandal or innuendo, of course—Mother's and Muttie's innately beautiful manners would never encompass that—but friendly gossip. They were Mistresses of Chat. Any neighbor was welcome to drop in for tea. No fuss, it was "just folks." At 3:55 P.M., Mother would scurry to the kitchen to the pale green Hoosier cabinet, grab the tea canisters (the Chinese black ones from a momentous trip to San Francisco), and set out the sky blue Lipton pot, a promotional giveaway made by the famous Red Wing potters. (It's a collector's item today.) She warmed the pot by running it under the hot water faucet, spooned in the tea, made sure the water had just come to a boil, and poured. I hustled some of Muttie's cookies or some graham crackers with her homemade icing onto a plate, while Mother waited a moment or two and then stirred the tea with a spoon in a graceful circular motion. It was exactly 4:00 P.M.

For our sun room teas Muttie was a steady baker, and store-bought cookies were hardly ever seen. Her favorites were Moravian ginger thins; she called them brown cookies—they were unevenly shaped and some were "a little brown at the edges." She baked them lightning fast: one bowl, and one cookie sheet, used again and again in quick succession, thus eliminating one more thing to wash afterwards. The point was to get something baked before the next household event swallowed up the time. The vanilla icing on purchased graham crackers was her neat compromise between store-bought and homemade: powdered sugar, warm milk, butter, and a dash of vanilla—all unmeasured, stirred up in a trice, and delicious when eaten a minute afterward, with the icing oozing out from all sides. And all who knew Muttie remember her big, soft, thick molasses cookies, always evoked with the same phrase: "She batted them out!"

The tea and cookies joined a hodgepodge of cups and saucers on an oval golden oak tea tray made by Papa, along with a sugar bowl, a small pitcher of milk (my favorite was a smiling jack-o'-lantern one, but if it wasn't clean, a juice glass would do), lemon slices, and a bowl for the slops. Next, Mother took a second pot, an ordinary Brown Betty, warmed it, and handed it over for me to carry. Nothing matched, all was serviceable; the rule for the teacups and cookie plates was no more than ten cents apiece at the dime store. It was homely in the best way: think of *Little Women* and you've got it.

The sky blue teapot held everything together. Perhaps it still does, as I have it to this day. It is, I think, the most perfect teapot ever. Every time I hold

Tea must be stored in the same way as a fine spice: in airtight tins, or ceramic jars (not glass), away from light and heat and especially from damp, the worst enemy of tea.

Seldom seen nowadays, slop basins—which look like large lidless sugar bowls—were standard on Victorian tea trays. At teatime, the drawing room doors were closed and the servants were dismissed, so it was practical, in the absence of plumbing, to have a vessel in which to dispose of cold, half-drunk tea.

it I marvel at its purity of line, so rounded and sweet, and at its blue color, so clean and sincere. No exaggerated handle swoops out in an enlarged arc, no cute pink or gray decorations spoil the simplicity of its surface. It swings easily in the hand, and pours perfectly without ever being unwieldy or awkward. It broadcasts a message of quiet confidence and strength. If it were a man, it would be a well-fed Norwegian ecumenical minister dressed in a perfectly fitting, light blue suit. You would trust this man.

The pot emptied fast; we never had a tea cozy until the fifties when Muttie knitted some in bright colors for friends and relations. The wild colors and mismatched plates we loved all blended together: the orange cookie plate with a fluted brown edge (the molasses cookies looked awfully good on that) and the fancy yellow one for the rare piece of revival cake, as Mother called it (stale cake dipped in milk and quickly warmed in the oven). This one was shaped like a pale yellow leaf with a raised pale red flower near the edge. This was a "downtown" plate, for visiting firemen: not a dime-store plate or a castoff, but a plate that had actually been bought *downtown,* in a glamorous department store.

When the tray was jam-packed with everything, we fairly *whisked* ourselves into the sun room. Get it *on,* and never mind the fusses and frills. The tea tray landed on the piano bench, and I set the empty Brown Betty pot teetering on the piano keys. When a few minutes had gone by, as we found our places, the contents of the sky blue Lipton pot were poured into that second pot. "Now it's fit to drink," Mother would say. The tea would have steeped to the moment of its fullest flavor before the process was stopped and it was decanted into the second pot, thus avoiding that brackish, bitter taste. How simple!

I realize now—after years of fooling around with tea balls, handheld strainers, tea-mote spoons, and spout filters—that these devices, no matter how noble their aim, make for distraction, and some actually get in the way. The balls and spoons wad up the tea, slowing circulation of water and thus inhibiting flavor. The strainers and spouts tempt one to forget the just-right moment to pour out the cups—or decant the whole into a warmed second pot. (A few leaves spilled into a cup add a bit of mysterious charm for tea-leaf reading—and will not alter the flavor in the cup.)

The tea ball and the tea infusion basket (that perforated, cylindrical device that is made to fit vertically into some pots) also appear to be wonderful inventions. But unless the leaf is allowed to whirl about, absorbing the water freely, that crucial moment when the oxygen releases the flavor of the tea is lost. Colored water is the result, and that's just what it tastes like. Because of this inadequate way of steeping, too many tea drinkers have never tasted real tea.

To have good tea, one must allow *the agony of the leaves* to take place. This phrase refers to the writhing, swirling action of the loose tea leaves immersed in boiling water. (The leaves may appear tormented and miserable, like autumn leaves in a storm, but they may also look dancing and fanciful; perhaps the coiner of this famous phrase was dyspeptic that day.) The term agony has been used in the tea trade for at least a century, and it is a wonder to me that it is not more popular. In any book on tea you will find it in the list of tea jargon—and what a phrase it is to play with! Without this watery "agony," nothing happens to the leaf. The flavor of the leaf is released at the molecular level by the oxygen-filled, life-giving water. Our brains need oxygen, and so does tea. That's a good way to remember to use fresh-drawn water that has *just* come to a rolling boil. Now the well-known catch phrase "Bring the pot to the kettle, not the kettle to the pot" begins to make sense. The instant the water is at the full rolling boil, *that* is the moment to pour—as mother used to tell me, "seconds count." After a time, you will learn to recognize the correct sound and propel yourself across the kitchen to do your on-the-spot job.

After a little stir with a spoon to circulate the tea fully, you must let it steep for three to five minutes. (Darjeelings usually take a little more time than other teas to achieve their flavor.) Then, just as Mother did, pour the tea from one pot into another one, straining it with a sieve if you are offended by a *few* leaves. (I'm not; I think of them like crumbs on the cake plate—just part of the experience.)

The moment I remembered this two-pot method was odd. I found myself in a remote country house where there was no tea ball and no strainer, and I'd improvised a proper tea by simply pouring the steeped tea into another pot. In a tiny little periscope flash to the past, I realized that I was making tea exactly the

way Muttie and Mother had. It made me smile. How could I have forgotten? It was so like them: practical, smart, not at all fussy. They both maintained a slickness and efficiency in their housekeeping: "Use it up, wear it out,/Make it do, or do without." A threadbare parsonage can teach you that. But Mother's housekeeping deviated somewhat and grew into a kind of enlightened sloppiness, a sort of casual ease and dispatch. Her attitude of "Oh, well, we'll just do it this way" was a relief from the almost relentless Germanic schedule that Muttie kept. In Muttie's world, supper was on the table at precisely 6:00 P.M. every night, the hour that God had clearly intended.

Basic and elementary as they were, those simple teas in the sun room were among the best teatimes in my life. On some afternoons in early spring, I would enter the house, my head spinning: the sky was *too* blue, the budding branches too quivery, and the high-pitched odor of the hyacinths and paper-whites exactly matched the headachey overstimulation I had carried home from school. The accumulated tension of spring made me long to fall into the oak chair, clutching my cup of tea. Within minutes, I was calmed; the gentle conversation, the milky tea, and the bit of carbohydrate all did their work. This calming effect remains one of the mysteries and delights of tea.

The tea I drank as a schoolgirl was cambric tea, so called because it is creamy white, the color of cambric (pronounced *came-brick*), the simple linen fabric that Victorian children's clothes were made of. "Scaled-down tea" would have been an excellent name for it, for that is just what it was: a lot of milk with a splash of tea and a spoonful of sugar or honey.

The actual brand of tea was usually Lipton's, of course, although we had

If you are cold tea will warm you; if you are depressed it will cheer you; if you are excited it will calm you.
—WILLIAM GLADSTONE
(1809–1898)

Cambric tea can be made in the cup or in the pot. The proportions should be about seven parts milk to one part tea, but a child will let you know soon enough what strength is preferred. Be generous with the sugar. I happen to think that green and herbal teas are not suitable for cambric tea, but as the ancient Chinese tea scholar Lu Yu said, "Goodness is a decision for the mouth to make."

Ty-Phoo (originally marketed as "An Invalid Tea") is a catchy transliteration of a Chinese word for "doctor." Swee-Touch-Nee, on the other hand, is a transliteration of the Russian word for "flowery," referring to the highly sought-after flowering leaves of the first crop (or first flush) of tea, which usually appears in April.

If you have several tins of tea, all half empty and a little stale, mix them all together! Often an intriguing and exciting flavor will emerge. This is called a Duke's Mixture.

other teas from time to time when Mother had been all the way downtown to get "something different." This meant Chinese tea from the one and only Chinese restaurant in town (The Nankin), or Ty-Phoo, or Swee-Touch-Nee ("The Aristocrat of Teas"), in its red-and-gold treasure chest. All the teas tasted pretty much the same to me, except for the Chinese one, which smelled exactly like everything else imported from China in those days—little dolls and fans, paper umbrellas and lanterns. It was probably an inferior jasmine. When there was only a little of each left in its canister, she would mix them all together in one. "Today we'll just do a Duke's Mixture," she would say. "It's always the best anyway."

Teas called "Duke's Mixtures" are created all over the world. The story behind the name is that the lazy butler of King George V (the boring one, who died in 1937) is supposed to have served a blend of the teas he had swept up off the floor after accidentally knocking over several containers of tea in the royal pantry. He served the new blend with perfect aplomb to his sovereign, who declared it the best tea he had ever drunk, and who, henceforth, would have no other. The butler had this impromptu blend duplicated by a tea blender, but the self-effacing king is said to have refused to allow it to bear his name, and it came to be named instead after an imaginary duke. The recipe remained a secret, as it does for many blends.

What is *not* a secret is how to make a pot of tea correctly with loose tea leaves, although to listen to some timid tea-baggers you would think it is the most difficult and mysterious thing in the world. Experiment with the blends, but not the method. Here are Mrs. Beeton's lucid instructions from her *Book of Household Management* (1859). The few minutes required are more than worth the effort:

> There is very little art in making good tea; if the water is boiling, and there is no sparing of the fragrant leaf, the beverage will almost invariably be good. The old-fashioned plan of allowing a teaspoonful to each person, and one over, is still practiced. Warm the teapot with boiling water; let it remain for two or three minutes for the vessel to

The color of the liquor—the tea term for the liquid tea in your cup—cannot guide you as to how a new tea will actually taste. Pale teas can be strong, and dark ones weak. Only when you are familiar with your new tea's individual color will its relative saturation tell you something about its strength.

become thoroughly hot, then pour it away. Put in the tea, pour in ½ to ¾ pint of *boiling* water, close the lid, and let it stand for the tea to draw from 5 to 10 minutes; then fill up the pot with water. The tea will be quite spoiled unless made with water that is actually *boiling,* as the leaves will not open, and the flavour not be extracted from them; the beverage will consequently be colourless and tasteless,—in fact, nothing but tepid water.

Instead of steeping the leaves for five to ten minutes in a little water, I pour in all the water at once just as Mother did, following the formula of one teaspoonful of tea per cup of water. In my experience, most teas have yielded their full flavor after just three to five minutes of steeping, not five to ten; and then I pour the tea into a second heated pot, again, just as Mother and Muttie used to do.

Home-made mixtures are popular. Mr. Twining's afternoon cup is one part Earl Grey to two parts English Breakfast. My morning cuppa is called Dragonmoon: one part superior-quality Assam to seven parts medium-quality Darjeeling.

RECIPES

Graham Cracker Sandwiches

If you want to create a little sun room tea in your world, a good way to start would be to follow Mrs. Beeton's formula for making the tea and grab a kid to help you make these vanilla-icing graham crackers. With a tiny amount of supervision a child of six could make these warm little treats.

The secret to making a good plain icing is to warm the milk; made with cold milk, the icing will taste unpleasantly metallic.

Pour 2 teaspoons milk into a heavy saucepan, add about ½ tablespoon butter, and stir over medium heat until the milk is warm and the butter is melted. Add 4 to 5 heaping tablespoons of powdered sugar and keep stirring until the icing is smooth. When it is thick enough (add more sugar if it is too thin), take the pot off the stove and add 3 or 4 drops of vanilla extract. Spread the icing lavishly on graham crackers and top each with another cracker.

Revival Cake

Take a stale, dry cake or piece of cake and completely immerse in whole milk for *exactly* one minute. Remove, place on a shallow baking pan, and put in a 250°F oven for about five minutes. If there is still a little milk on the baking pan around the cake, leave it in another minute or two until the milk is completely absorbed. Serve topped with jam, a few shaved nuts, or coconut. "Not a meal to invite a man to," as Samuel Johnson would say, but just right for a sun room teatime.

Muttie's One-Bowl Brown Cookies

MAKES ABOUT 6 DOZEN COOKIES

*The title on the card in Muttie's recipe box reads "Brown Cookies (good)," and the list of
ingredients says only "Spices," since she assumed, I guess, that everyone knows what spices
to use for good brown cookies. These are tricky because the dough is thin and tends to tear
easily. They inevitably turn out misshapen and lopsided, but in my view this makes them
more authentic.*

¼ cup butter, room tempera-
    ture (I'm sure Muttie used
    lard or bacon fat)
½ cup sugar
½ cup brown sugar
1 egg
2½ cups all-purpose flour
2 teaspoons baking powder
⅛ teaspoon nutmeg

1¼ teaspoons cinnamon
¼ teaspoon cloves
½ teaspoon ginger
½ cup molasses (use dark, full-
    flavored molasses)
1½ tablespoons apple cider
    vinegar
¼ teaspoon baking soda

In a large bowl, cream together the butter, sugar, and brown sugar with an electric beater. Make a well in the center, break the egg into it, and beat until frothy.
Sprinkle the flour, baking powder, and spices into the bowl (as if sowing seeds),
distributing them as evenly as possible. Stir it all together vigorously and make
another well in the center. Put a measuring cup in the well (Muttie used a pretty
old cup without a handle), and stir together the molasses and vinegar in the cup.
Add the baking soda to the cup; the mixture will foam up. Empty the cup into
the well and stir thoroughly into the surrounding dough.

    Put the bowl, *uncovered,* in the refrigerator, and leave it there overnight; or
if you can't wait, put it in the freezer for about half an hour instead.

    Preheat the oven to 325°F. Grease a cookie sheet (a thin, old-fashioned one, not the double-layered kind). Take out the bowl and, with floured hands, lift out the dough and put it on a floured board. With quick, light strokes, roll out the dough to a thickness of about ⅛ inch. If the dough is too sticky to roll out smoothly, add more flour. (This cookie can absorb a lot of flour without harm to the flavor.) Cut out cookies with a 2½- to 3-inch round cookie or biscuit cutter. Place them on the greased cookie sheet and bake for 15 minutes. Watch them carefully. When they are done, take them off the cookie sheet with a spatula and cool them on cake racks. (Muttie cooled hers on pieces of brown paper or newspaper.)

Molasses Cookies, or Muttie's Big Cookies

MAKES ABOUT 30 COOKIES

On the other side of the recipe card for Brown Cookies is this recipe for Molasses Cookies, which also calls for unspecified spices. I've used cinnamon and cloves because that is the common combination most molasses cookie recipes call for. These cookies do not taste sensational until they have been allowed to ripen for two or three days to bring out their full flavor and soft, chewy texture. They are more than excellent with a glass of cold milk—or a cup of milky tea.

¾ cup butter (*not* margarine), room temperature	2 cups all-purpose flour
1 cup sugar	½ teaspoon salt
1 egg	1 teaspoon ground cinnamon
¼ cup dark molasses	¼ to ½ teaspoon ground cloves
	Sugar

In a large bowl, cream together the butter and sugar until very smooth. Make a well in the center, break the egg into it, beat until frothy, and then stir into the butter and sugar. Add the molasses and mix thoroughly.

In another bowl, combine the flour, salt, and spices, mixing well. Add the

dry ingredients to the molasses mixture and stir until well blended. Chill it in the refrigerator for a few hours if you have time, or slip the bowl into the freezer, uncovered, for half an hour.

Preheat the oven to 375°F. Lightly grease a baking sheet. Take the bowl of dough out of the refrigerator or freezer and with a teaspoon, dig out spoon-size balls (about an inch in diameter). Roll the balls in a saucer filled with ordinary granulated sugar and place them on the baking sheet about two inches apart.

Bake for about 8 to 10 minutes. When done, cool them on a cake rack or a large plate. Store in a cookie jar or tin.

Chapter Two

THE FACULTY FOLLIES
TEA PARTY

Before the war came—a time that was safe and stable and genteel—my family and I lived in a house on a prominent corner of the Faculty Grove, a wooded gentle slope of hills overlooking Minneapolis. The Grove, as we always called it, owned by the University of Minnesota, became a sanctuary where only faculty members could build. We faculty kids felt that we were "quite a number" (the 1940s phrase for "cool") because of this idyllic place, and we were just short of being obnoxious.

In the seventh grade my friends and I thought *Anne of Green Gables* was for dopes; we were enamored of Greer Garson, the Brontës, Ravel's *Bolero,* and Tabu lipstick—when we were allowed to wear it. My best friend, Rutabaga Ruth—sometimes called Ruthie, Pooph, or Poophiegay—lived in a house across the street, exactly forty-four running steps from my back door. She was short and stubby; I was tall and what we used to call "strikingly thin." My nickname was Lemon Helen, and we made quite a pair. We had no boyfriends. "Dates" were unheard of things to our parents, and we pretended we didn't care.

Focused, high-minded intellectuals were as common as dirt to us. Our

fathers, both professors at "the U" (there was only one), were dignified, awe-inspiring gentlemen just a step away from the Founders of the University—as revered as ministers a century before. I heard my father say "damn" just once in my entire life (a stovepipe fell, soot everywhere, and it was the morning of my confirmation).

Calling cards were still sometimes used by the senior members of the faculty, and velvet-caped ladies and their escorts drifted from house to house for progressive dinner parties, for which white-aproned maids were hired if there was no live-in help. When my parents hired Mrs. Paulsson for these occasions, Rutabaga and I could hardly wait for her to arrive at our front door wearing her large gray apron. We knew what lay underneath. After the guests arrived, the gray apron would be removed, revealing a large presentable white one, just in case a guest *should* catch sight of her in the kitchen. We exulted at the moment when, all in a sweat, she would whip that one off, exposing a third frilly apron, a tiny island of white in the sea of black sateen that covered her ample front. She would then sashay into the dining room to serve, summoned by the lightbulb activated when my mother's searching foot found the floor-level button by her chair. (It was a greatly admired scheme—so discreet, and *such* an improvement over the old bell system.)

The Grove was known as a "lovely place to live." And it was—both leafy and substantial. On Sundays outsiders would drive through just to look. Rutabaga and I thought of ourselves as sophisticates who, by the vagaries of fate, just *happened* to be attending a demonstration high school on the University of Minnesota campus. In fact, we were guinea pig faculty brats. Our English class had seven students and thirteen quivering practice teachers lavishing attention on every literary conceit that spiraled out of our mouths.

About this time, we discovered that our mothers' friends had funny names, and we dedicated ourselves to reciting them in unison at the slightest lull in the repartee. All were members of the prestigious Faculty Women's Club, or F.W.C. (The initials might as well have stood for Faculty *Wives'* Club, for only a few of its members were on the faculty themselves.) Though we jeered a little at the ladies, I think even then we had a sense of the bubbly camaraderie they enjoyed.

Nothing stood in the way of those meetings! A paragraph in the tiny one-volume *History of the F.W.C., 1911–1914* tells it gracefully:

> Newcomers to the University of Minnesota from schools that had a
> women's club on the campus missed the easy and pleasant avenue to
> friendship which such a club provided. They spoke of the advantages
> of a campus club for women to any and all who would listen, and the
> idea took root.

The tone reflects the stately, measured pace of the time—and sweetly masks the determination of the group to get together, to make friends, to belong.

The funny, fascinating names poured forth on the homeward-bound street-car as Rutabaga and I matched the rhythm of the wheels with our chant. Plump Genevieve Bade (pronounced "body," as in "We-don't-talk-about-that-dear") and skinny Ila Vold were always paired. Both had winter windows stuffed with African violets and both were excellent cooks. Mrs. Bade, a champion club woman, would arrive home after a meeting, and, *with hat and gloves still on,* guiltily set the table, turn on the oven, and dab Old World Dutch Furniture Polish on the chair posts. Then, quite relaxed, she would ascend the stairs for a change of clothes, confident of her homey stage setting. Later she'd descend for a leisurely preparation of dinner that could be scandalously late, at seven, or eight, or even nine o'clock; meanwhile hubby, just home from the chemistry lab, would have sniffed and peered around the house and satisfied himself that all was right with the world.

I love to think of Mrs. Bade as a Helen Hokinson cartoon, her bird-shaped felt hat perched at an angle, her gloved hands daub-daubing the furniture. The caption reads: "Pant, pant . . . George will be here any minute!" The wide-eyed drama of it all—her intrepid girth whirling about the room as she covered up, having sweetly cheated on the old man with an afternoon of heavy indulgence improving herself with The Ladies.

Next, our fingers tapping a drum roll, came Florence Rumbaugh (Mathematics), a rumbling name with the accent on the *rum*. Then Mattie Bell Gabler

(History) and Ruby Glockler (Chemistry). All those glottals speak for themselves. Both Mattie Bell and Ruby were cheerful, bustling wonders. Etiquette in The Grove dictated that if one was acquainted with the lady mentioned, there was no need to attach her husband's—or her own—identifying department. If not, it was used for quick placement in the pecking order—not that anyone would ever have admitted to the existence of such an un-Christian practice. As a small child, I was so accustomed to this way of speaking that when I heard there was a woman on the faculty named Phyllis French (Physics), I assumed she was so smart that she was in two departments. But a plexus of my brain nerve endings fused, never to be used again, when she married her noted colleague George Frier and became Phyllis French Frier (Physics) (Physics).

Here we gave ourselves a big pause, before plunging on to Mrs. Jules Piccard (Oceanography). She was a real vegetarian, ate something called wheat germ, and wore her hair (loose!) in a ponytail. She and her husband were French; Jules and his twin brother, Jean (Astronomy), were a curiosity. One went up in a balloon and the other down in a bathysphere. We called them the Up 'n' Down Piccards. Their hair was long (down to their collars!), their eyes were wild, they never wore neckties, and they always strode or darted, never walked. *Exotic* is the only word. On any college campus today they would be overlooked, but in 1942 things were different. They were *not* dignified.

For mellifluousness, our arms floating up in balletic gestures, we added Ola Mae Vaughan (General College) and Ethel Hellig (Physical Education). Rutabaga always said the names and departments of this pair as fast as possible for the proper effect. We used long vowels and a lilting inflection for Mrs. Ancel Keyes (the wife of a nationally known scholar). We shifted to the lower register and began practicing pliés as we roared out Anna Augusta Von Helmholtz Phalen (she wore a red wig) and Elvira Gil d'Lamadrid (which rhymes with "mama-grid"). August professors themselves, they had names that inspired, just as they should, fear, dread . . . and stifled laughter.

Now, chins down and torsos braced, we boomed out, in a crescendo of energy and authority, "Mrs. Frank Ger-r-r-rout!" the long, hard midwestern "r" held interminably. Her age, her station, her place as a senior member in my mother's pack, her husband's standing in the Geology Department, her dark presence, her heavy felt hat with one center headlight ornament glowing over her pince-nez glasses, her sausage torso encircled by a tiny belt and tarnished rhinestone buckle made her, to put it mildly, impressive. Beside her, my mother's junior friends (who were called by their first names) came off as shameless, hatless ladies with their dainty frocks, polished nails, and glistening marcelled hair. In a faded photograph, Mrs. Grout resembles a lumpy leaden statue surrounded by shimmering silver sea birds.

The name we loved the most we saved until the very end. A seamless and luminous name, a romantic favorite: Opal Gruener (Physics). Part of its charm was the way other ladies said it, especially the Norwegians: "Opal . . ." (head up, bottom teeth protruding); a pause, then (chin down, eyes looking up), ". . . Grooner." It was said in a tone of utmost approval, almost adoration. When she pronounced her own last name, it was in almond-shaped, musical tones that broke enchantingly midway through the first fluty vowel. Her smooth, dark, wavy, marcelled hair, pulled back into a Wallis Simpson neck roll, delineating her white brow, was a welcome relief from the side-parted, post-Wellesley bobs of the others. She wore a size eight (a *real* size eight: before the manufacturers started lowering the numbers to make us tiny). Her oval face, translucent skin, and pretty pink and white fingernails created an image that her acolytes Rutabaga Ruth and Lemon Helen worshiped, ever from afar.

❧   ❧   ❧

Each year the ladies of the F.W.C. put forth their best efforts in a specially written playlet, "The Faculty Follies," costumed reluctantly by the Theatre Department. All F.W.C. sections became involved, even Child Care (Mother's section), the Pen Club, and the stylish Bridge Club. A lavish tea party followed the play, and in 1942, Rutabaga and

I were asked to serve. We were honored and a little awed, but we maintained our image by rolling our eyes and looking disgusted. I don't think we succeeded.

Besides recruiting us, Mother's assignments for the tea were to bring four jelly rolls, which she made with more ease than anyone in her circle (her recipe card's last line reveals the secret: "Don't play with it!"), date bars, and her famous tea concentrate, her party-saver, as she called it. It was made the day before, on the samovar principle—diluted to the proper strength with boiling water just before serving. Mother's concentrate even made it into the faculty cookbook, *A Curriculum for Cooks,* published by the University of Minnesota Hospital Auxiliaries. (The title was fun to say over and over—the faster, the funnier.) The next day, in the Student Union Ballroom kitchen, she poured the concentrate into warmed silver urns to about one-quarter full. Then the urns were filled with boiling water and taken to the table in the ballroom. The hostess and pourer needed only to depress the little handle and make merry small talk to the burbling ladies. "It was slick!" my mother would say, slapping her palms together, one hand sailing forward like a racehorse bursting out of a gate.

Men loved the date bars, especially during the war, when chocolate was rationed and scarce. Even if it had been available, no one would have thought of using it for tea party refreshments; it was saved for the "soldier boys." Rarely, someone would make chocolate chip cookies from a thin scored bar of chocolate broken into bits—but the cookies would be dismissed, and the brownies, too, with a righteous sneer: "*Well,* you might as well make *candy!*"

When the great day came close, we helped Mother make the date bars on a late December afternoon, rolling them in powdered sugar that reminded us of the falling snow outside. We took samples on paper plates to the neighbors, using the new and faddish royal blue tissue paper, dashing out from the steamy kitchen into the snow under a sky we called evening-in-Paris blue, after the famous frosty deep blue perfume bottle. My mother looked like a seraph with her blond topknot and wispy curls haloing her face. It was heavenly.

> The samovar, a marvelous invention from the great heart of Russia, keeps water freshly boiling (or nearly freshly) in a large urn, ready to combine with concentrated tea liquor warming in a teapot on top of the urn. Turn the spigot at the bottom of the urn, fill your glass cup, add a small amount of tea from the pot above, to taste, take a slice of lemon or a cube of sugar between your teeth, and imbibe.

The pre-Follies tension started to build—who was to make the Checker-board Sandwiches? Thankfully they were not our assignment. Mrs. Jane Bardeen took them on, as she was famous for her deft and esoteric cooking. She had once hollowed out oranges, made sherbet out of the pulp and put it back in the "shells," froze them (no mean feat considering the tiny freezer compartments of those days), garnished them with sprigs of mint, and stood back. Sensation. Nothing quite like that had ever been seen, at least not in our provincial circles. (The Bardeens wore *tweeds* and were from Back East.)

The impressive Checkerboards were made from loaves of interlocked strips of whole wheat and white bread bound together with a cheese spread or mayon-naise. Like much of the festive food of the forties, they tasted ordinary but looked spectacular. Looks, in the forties, were nearly everything.

When the big day finally came, we helped Mother carefully load the boxes of date bars, the bottles filled with dark tea concentrate, and the cookie sheets bearing the jelly rolls (each one resting on wax paper under a white tea towel) into the back seat of our "old bus"—a 1938 robin's-egg blue De Soto—and drove to the ballroom entrance of the Student Union.

When we arrived, already nervy and excited, we found the room almost filled with Cuban-heeled women setting up and click-clicking about. We took in The Ladies. Mrs. Grout steered her way through the crowd, her flat maroon hat sailing along like the top deck of a small ship; Ola Mae Vaughan sparkled by in her rimless glasses, looking friendly and approachable in an aqua gabardine suit and a lace blouse; and the peerless Opal Gruener glided through, our only fashion plate as usual, in a figure-hugging pale, pale lavender wool crepe suit and a tiny black satin twisted-ribbon hat that the Duchess of Windsor might have chosen for a little at-home tea party. *Ahh.*

As the actual party began, the great crush of talcum-powdered ladies formed a nearly impenetrable barrier around the urns of tea. They wore rayon crepe and were piled high in their foundation garments, the one-piece corset and girdle popular then. I loved the shiny, overpressed crepe suits, the sequined corsages, the furry hats, the frizzy hair, the fingernail polish, the smell of Evening in Paris (and the occasional whiff of Tweed!). Would I grow up to wear such outfits?

It is said that 98 percent of all tea drunk in the United States (except herbals) is black. Is this evidence of an industrial conspiracy against green tea, or is black tea so popular because its assertive taste and high caffeine content give the biggest lift to body and soul?

Black tea's flavor comes from fermentation and oxidation of the juice in the leaf while it is rolled, muti-lated, and wrung. Afterward the tea leaf is said to be "caramelized"—an old tea term. After firing (drying), it is a shrunken, wiry, twisted, rolled, desiccated, mummified thing, but it is poised to release its glories.

In case we had to say something when serving our Ladies, we had looked up Emily Post on the subject of genteel conversation while pouring (hot chocolate, in this case, but we picked up the tone):

> It is merest good manners on [the pourer's] part to make a few pleasant remarks. Very likely when someone asks for chocolate, she says, "How nice of you! I have been feeling very neglected at my end. Everyone seems to prefer tea." After an observation or two about the weather, or the beauty of the china or how good the little cakes look, or the sandwiches taste, the guest finishes the chocolate.

But we never had a moment for our lines. The ladies pushed and persevered and we nearly panicked. No one could get to our date bars! And complaints were heard that no one could get to the tea! As the tension mounted, we kept stealing back to the kitchen like bandits and sneaking shot after shot of tea to propel us forward. With or without milk, with or without lemon; sometimes we gulped it lukewarm. Any way would do; we *needed* it!

Back at the tea table, we suddenly saw Mrs. Jules Piccard (of the Down Piccards) darting out of the crowd, her ponytail pulled back, bright-eyed and pointy-nosed and looking like a hungry fish. She was crossing the floor (in what? were those *summer* sandals?). She had two small pots, one in each hand, filled with freshly brewed tea. Somehow she had managed to find loose tea leaves and brew them. Her behavior seemed undignified, even to me. "This is better tea! Here we have the *agony of the leaves!* Won't you have some?" Her agony tea wasn't selling, although a few timid souls partook. We avoided the agony; it seemed too foreign. But the expression intrigued me (like everything about Mrs. Piccard) and vaguely unsettled me. The phrase stayed in my mind.

We continued to serve the barrier reef of ladies, making slow headway. The crowd pressed round us, everyone balancing her teacup and plate and speaking squeakily at the top of her vocal register. That high-pitched tone, almost a shriek, I now realize was the huge sound of a roomful of unrecognized egos and stifled talent. Sweating and swerving to avoid collisions, I felt the tea beginning

*I*magine you were given the assignment of making a rather bland, nearly ripe, just-picked apricot as assertive and flavorful as it could possibly be. If you cut the apricot in pieces, set it out in the sun to blacken, bring it inside and spray it with a fine mist of water, and repeat this procedure, then cut it up in smaller pieces, mash them, sliver them, and twist and roll them, and finally squish and pack them, you would produce some version of a dried apricot that has a lot more flavor than a fresh one. This, in the broadest of terms, is what turns a green tea leaf into black tea.

When freshly boiling water pours over these twisted, rolled-up leaves, all that stored-up flavor is released. The swirling and writhing of the leaves mark the moment when this happens. The moment is called *the agony of the leaves.* The plantation owners and workers, packers, buyers, shippers, and tea people the world over wait for this crucial moment when tea comes back to life.

to take effect. I was experiencing my first real tea "high," what some term "the marvelous tea sweat."

Clutching our new rayon-and-cotton stockings up, and wrenching our new garter belts down, our abdomens tightly constricted, we fielded the whole mob. Once Marc Connelly, the author of *Green Pastures,* summoned from New York for a speech at an F.W.C. banquet, took one look at the ladies through the curtain, put his hand to his forehead and murmured, "One thousand girdles . . . I can't do it," and had to be led to the podium. We felt somewhat the same way, but we fielded, we feinted, we responded, we joked—and suddenly we realized we were having a *spectacular* time! Everyone seemed a little bigger, prettier, more vital, kinder, funnier; the very air seemed to expand; humor and nonsense were applauded, clumsiness faded. We belonged!

When the affair was over at last, I raced back to the kitchen to sneak more slices of jelly roll as Rutabaga, ever the dutiful, served the exhausted ladies. Finally, we sighed contentedly and went home on the intercampus trolley, a bright yellow streetcar that shuttled between the main and the agricultural campuses. It was as perfect as the one in *Meet Me in St. Louis,* because it had an open platform at the back where one could lean out, catch the breezes, and touch the branches of the trees at the edge of The Grove. Skippy, the lone conductor, knew our names—he must have memorized hundreds, both the professors' and the students'. We felt like privileged young princesses in our private railroad car. Actually, that's just what we were.

(Skippy's story is a sad one. Hugh [Skipper] Spencer had a photographic memory. He aspired to the bar and passed, we heard, the first time with a perfect score. This was so unbelievable that he was assumed to have cheated and was disqualified. In those days—the late twenties—lawsuits were considered ungentlemanly, and he felt he had no appeal. He chose to work near the academic world and used his mental gift to delight and impress thousands of faculty and students. Though decades could pass, Skippy would greet the returning prodigals by their first and last names.)

The next day, we learned what had happened after we left. The incident was to become famous in faculty women's circles. Some workmen had appeared, dressed in their customary white overalls and caps, and asked if they could begin to fix the radiators. In a grand mood, the tall and usually taciturn Mrs. Henry A. (Anton) Erikson (Physics) said, "Yes, of course," with a gracious smile, and asked if they would like some leftover treats. To her complete amazement, instead of the reply she expected—"Why no, you just go on now"—they answered, "Why yes, we would." Very few workmen spoke that way, especially not the Scandinavian retired farmers who made up the janitorial staff. Stunned, Mrs. Erikson double-timed it back to the kitchen, banged the door behind her, and wide-eyed, panted, "Omigosh, what'll we do *now?*" Explosion. Laughter. Frantic handwringing and scurrying. Emergency! Here was a crisis of a proper proportion.

They threw themselves into the task and produced something, nobody remembers what; it wasn't important. The story became legend—my mother reenacting it year after year, with each detail in place. It was always received by the ladies with gales of laughter. A huge joke, what a caper! "To think of the predicament—" "Imagine, just *imagine* getting caught that way!" For me, more than any other story, this incident shows the gentility, the isolation, and the unused energies of those bright, unfulfilled women.

At home that evening, returning the hated garter belt to Mother's dresser, I looked past the tiny balcony out the window next to her pale peach chintz-skirted dressing table to the lights of the city below. I saw the Foshay Tower, our one and only skyscraper, and as I listened to the train whistles echoing from the flats below (a sound that still enchants me), I was swept back to the ballroom. My very soul had opened up. The ladies had talked to me as friends, as *colleagues*—an extremely important word for a faculty kid. I had become elevated and larger than before.

Magnanimity crept into my soul. My role in high school as the class clown, the unattractive, unsexy, tall "character" had begun to fade, and I thought with new sweetness about the rich socialite girls I had always envied. They had a full complement of at least ten cashmere sweaters per girl! (I managed one short-sleeved one by graduation.) I forgave the two boys who never asked me for a date, James Marvin and Robert Setzer (whose names are still fraught with sexy tweed-jacket allure for me), even though they knew they were the only two boys in the class tall enough to ask me. And I definitely forgave Bob Pirsig (later of *Zen and the Art of Motorcycle Maintenance* fame) for sneering at me as I took Algebra for the third time around. After all, he was just a shy chess fanatic. All were forgiven, all seen in their best lights.

I slid down the banister to the kitchen for a large cup of tea with plenty of milk, and snuck one last date bar. Its soaring, center-of-the-tongue sweetness matched my glowing mood. My heightened perception, the headiness of it all, made the meanness flow out of me. We were all in this together, weren't we? A marvelous sense of well-being and trust in my fellows, a feeling of budding creativity, of harmony and love, simply took over. I was powerless to find reasons to be unhappy or to feel like I had been shortchanged by the world.

In Minnesota, it is typically assumed that one is honest, responsible, faithful, accurate, clean, neat, good-tempered, *even*-tempered, obedient, modest, selfless, patient, kind, helpful, magnanimous, fair, tolerant, capable, punctual, polite, and that one *always* has clean fingernails—just for starters. The main question beneath all that is, what are *you* going to do for the world? In such an atmosphere of expectation, to be relaxed and filled with joy over a simple act of helping serve was a marvelous, marvelous relief.

Was this what a tea could do? Was this what helping serve was all about? Could it be this simple?

I began dimly to perceive myself as an adult. Of course, I would never manage the hose (seams straight), the slip, the foundation garment (or the girdle), the damp dress shields clinging to my armpits, the blouse with the bow, the suit, the zipper that stuck, the corsage (on the left), the earrings (clip-on, of course), the lapel pin, the purse, the pressed handkerchief *in* the purse, the gloves, the hat, the veil, the powdered nose, the soft Tangee lipstick. (I was right; at forty I was braless.) But I did feel a certain letting go of petty considerations. It seemed it might, just might be possible to be fine and open and generous, to be a big substantial soul—just possible. My cheeks began to burn bright in a reprise of the afternoon's triumph.

I floated up the stairs to my bedroom and looked in the mirror. My eyes were larger and more lustrous than I had ever seen them. I crawled into bed and started smiling. I felt deeply encouraged.

RECIPES

Ballroom Date Bars

MAKES ABOUT 40 DATE BARS

A child of five can make these. One of the blessings of this recipe is the pared-down ingredients list, leaving full sway to the major elements. The lavish amounts of nuts and dates and the unbeaten egg make it chewy and delightful, not to mention easy to make. Mother (Viola Buchta—not a bad name either) was famous for these bars.

> 1½ cups cut-up dates (right out of the box)
> 1½ cups chopped walnuts
> 3 teaspoons baking powder
> 3 eggs (not beaten)
> 3 tablespoons flour (that's correct, 3 tablespoons)
> 1½ cups powdered sugar, plus more for rolling the bars in after
>   baking

Grease an 8×13-inch pan. In a large bowl, mix the ingredients in the order given. Be gentle and do not overmix; these need to rise. Spread the mixture in the greased pan and bake at 375°F for 30 minutes. While still warm, cut into squares. Roll in powdered sugar.

The Best Jelly Roll

Growing up, I was nudged out of the kitchen entirely by my grandmother, who managed our household, so as an adolescent I bolted in the opposite direction and only allowed myself to be cooked *for.* My

brother, a tease of professional caliber, gave me Irma Rombauer's *The Joy of Cooking* as a joke. I ignored it until I got married.

Forty-five years later, on page 572 of the 1946 edition, the jelly roll recipe emerged, as if by magic, with a note in my mother's neat and sprightly hand: "Use lard to grease pan; use center rack at 375°." Good advice. Mrs. Rombauer's note above the recipe is an example of her deft literary charm:

> This was the first cake I ever attempted, "so many years ago." It was then an old recipe. It is interesting to note that it has held its own as the standard roll cake without the slightest change through all this time.

Rolled cakes; chocolate "Lincoln Logs"; lemon, custard, and even ice-cream-filled rolls were madly popular in the thirties, forties, fifties, and even into the sixties. Failure or competence in producing jelly rolls was a definite indicator of a cook's prowess. For a bride, the first test was scorch-free bacon and toast, then a presentable pie, and later an angel or sponge cake. But jelly roll was the ultimate measuring stick. Many cooks of my generation have a roasting pan known as the jelly roll pan. As a kid, my hopes rose when I was asked to scramble around in the bottom compartment of the Hoosier cabinet for the jelly roll pan, only to have them dashed when I found it, finally, in the ice box, filled with a horrid old roast.

Cake failure was a serious matter. The 1944 *Better Homes and Gardens Cook Book*'s comments on the subject are refreshingly blunt:

REASONS FOR ANGEL AND SPONGE CAKE FAILURE

- *Coarse Texture*—Underbeaten egg whites. Insufficient blending of ingredients. Too slow an oven.
- *Tough Cake*—Too hot an oven—high temperature toughens egg protein. Not enough sugar. Overmixing.
- *Cracks in Crust*—Overbeaten egg whites. Too much sugar. Too hot an oven.

- *Sticky Crust*—Too much sugar. Insufficient baking.
- *Heavy Sticky Layer at Bottom*—Underbeaten egg yolks or insufficient mixing of egg yolk with other ingredients.
- *Undersized Cake*—Either underbeaten or overbeaten egg whites. Overmixing, causing loss of air. Too large a pan. Too hot an oven. Removed from pan too soon.

A list for the advanced student, as the textbooks used to say. One can imagine a great cloud of clamoring cooks pelting questions at the editors, and the carefully weighed responses.

The memory of the white light surrounding the pretty, wholesome faces of my aunt and mother as they leaned over the cake at the crucial moment when it is inverted onto the tea towels and dredged with fluffy powdered sugar inspired me to gather to my bosom all the jelly roll recipes I could find. And it's nice to discover that Mrs. Rombauer was right—the only deviations are as small as one-half teaspoon more or less of vanilla, and one egg added. A classic is always reassuring.

These instructions come from the 1944 *Better Homes and Gardens Cook Book* and are more explicit than those given by Mrs. Rombauer, who assumed the reader had enough sense to beat the egg yolks until "thick and lemon-colored." The ingredients list in both books is exactly the same.

4 egg yolks	¾ cup cake flour
¾ cup sugar	¼ teaspoon salt
½ teaspoon vanilla extract	1 teaspoon baking powder
4 egg whites	

Beat egg yolks until thick and lemon-colored; gradually add ¼ cup sugar and the vanilla extract. Beat egg whites until almost stiff; gradually add remaining ½ cup sugar and beat until very stiff. Fold yolks into whites, then add sifted dry ingredients, folding in carefully. Bake in waxed-paper-lined 10½×15-inch jelly roll pan in moderate oven (375°F) 12 minutes. Loosen sides and turn out onto towel sprinkled with confectioners' sugar. Remove waxed paper. Trim crusts. Roll quickly with fresh sheet of waxed paper on inside of roll. Wrap in sugared towel; cool. Unroll; remove paper; spread with jelly or other favorite filling. Roll again. Sprinkle top with a modest amount of powdered sugar as a finishing touch. Cover with towel again if cake is to be transported.

Checkerboard Sandwiches

This recipe is taken word for word from the Better Homes and Gardens Holiday Cook Book. *Good bakery bread and a sharp serrated knife are essential to success in this venture, as well as good mayonnaise and/or a tasty cheese spread. Pimento-flavored fillings were very popular.*

Remove crusts from 2 unsliced sandwich loaves—1 white, 1 whole wheat. From each loaf, cut 6 lengthwise slices ½-inch thick (or have bread sliced at the bakery). This will make 3 Ribbon Loaves.

Use Cheese Butter to put 4 long slices of bread together, alternating 2 whole wheat and 2 white. Make 3 loaves. Wrap in foil, plastic wrap, or waxed paper; chill; slice crosswise to make thin "ribbons."

Make Ribbon Loaves. Cut in 6 *lengthwise* slices. Put 4 slices together, alternating colors, to make checkerboard. Wrap and chill. Slice *crosswise.* Two Ribbon Loaves make 3 Checkerboards.

CHEESE BUTTER

Mix one 5-ounce jar sharp spreading cheese and ¼ pound soft butter.

PARSLEY BUTTER

Blend ¼ cup soft butter, 1½ tablespoons finely chopped parsley, and ½ teaspoon lemon juice.

A good-quality Darjeeling makes a wonderful concentrate. At one tea party I was challenged to identify a delicious black tea, and couldn't. It turned out to be good old Lipton's loose supermarket tea! One secret to making tasty tea is to buy from a large, heavily trafficked supermarket where frequent turnover of stock assures you of freshness.

Mother's Tea Concentrate

Here is the recipe, verbatim from the Faculty Women's Club's A Curriculum for Cooks.

Tea Concentrate

Viola Buchta (Physics)

1 cup tea
1 quart boiling water

Steep for 7 minutes. Strain and place in glass container. Makes 50 cups of tea. Concentrate may be made ahead and stored in refrigerator for later use. Allow 1 tablespoon concentrate for each cup of tea. (A big help at "tea parties." One simply adds concentrate to boiling water according to size of pot and strength of tea desired.)

Any kind of tea that pleases can be used for a concentrate: Earl Grey, Jasmine, a fruit-flavored tea, or a favorite black tea. Ceylon, English Breakfast, Keemun, Nilgiri, or black Yunnan will all do; the Ceylon and English Breakfast are favored for "regular black tea" that most folks want for a large tea party. The assertive nature of both these teas almost guarantees a vigorous concentrate and, thus, a satisfying tea.

Boil the water in a large nonreactive pot and pour through a large strainer into glass jars. If the tea turns cloudy, a zap of hot water will clear it. Cap the jars and store overnight. They need not be refrigerated, but can be if you desire.

Chapter Three

IRISH HONEYMOON

I grew up, I went to college, I tried my hand at the theater, I sang and danced. After a time, I settled down to teaching school and, in 1960, was married. I taught for two more years and my husband finished his M.A.; we then decided to sell our graduate school furniture and take off on a honeymoon in Europe. We would spend all our savings, buy a car in Germany, and stay abroad for an entire year. Our parents were ashen-faced over our mad plan. My mother had to sit down when she heard that we had arranged our sailing date.

By the fall of 1963, we were in Dublin, staying in a quiet, clean, separate-tables boarding house run by a woman known only as Maude. Here we were Irished up, learning all about Ireland and the Irish, and most of all, about Irish food and drink. In one corner of the sparsely furnished white dining room in the basement sat a range on which a pot of oatmeal appeared to be perpetually simmering. I had been a fan of oatmeal all my life, but now I was in Olympian oatmeal territory. Maude served it with a selection of additions: brown sugar, heavy cream, butter, currants, and black raisins. It was smooth, thick, and formidable. With it, she served the tea she served with everything else: Barry's of Cork. After

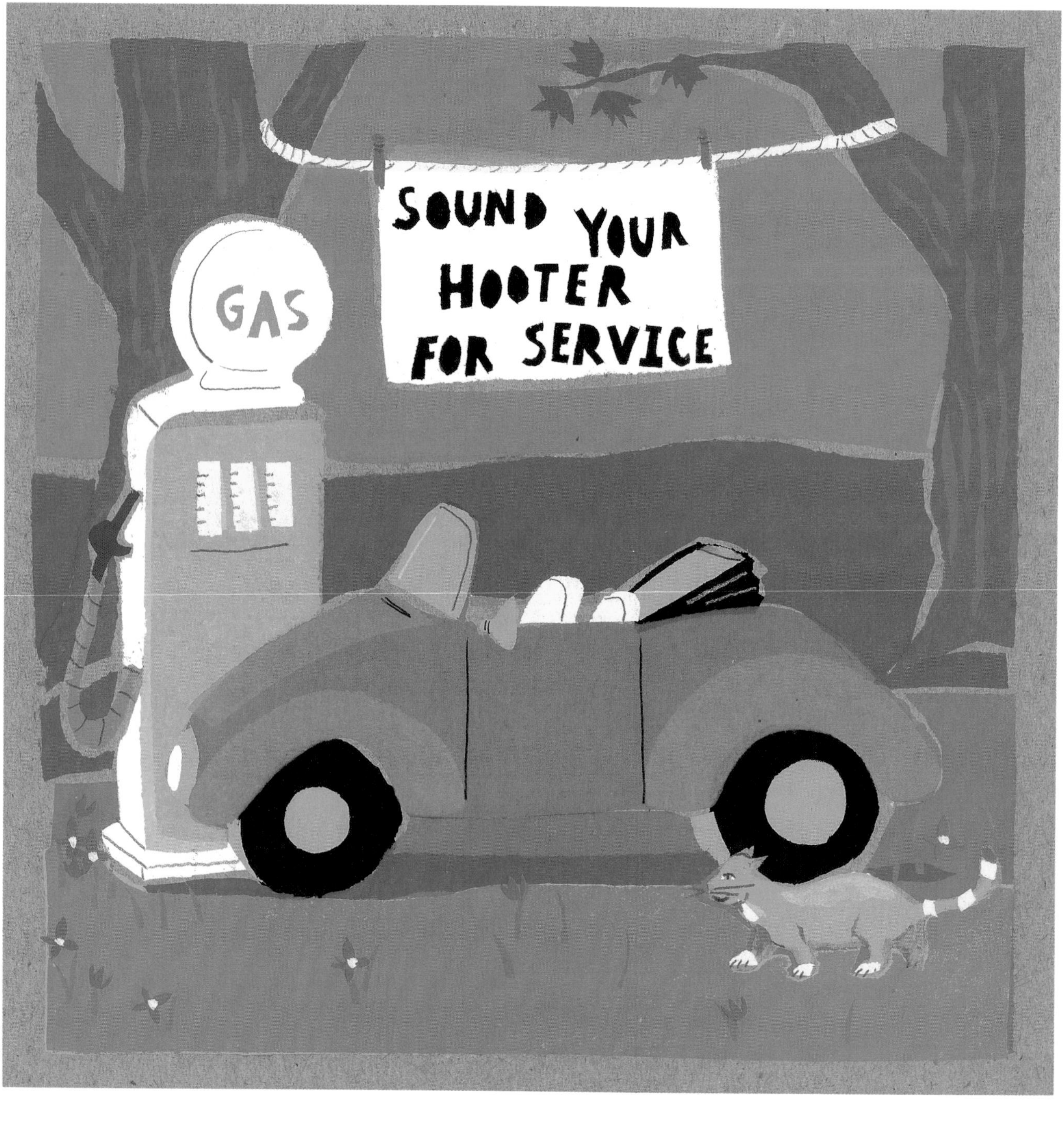
SOUND YOUR
HOOTER
FOR SERVICE
GAS

we had taken tea we understood why Mr. Barry had won the Empire Challenge Cup for Tea Blending. Barry's tea is still the biggest, boldest, roundest, toastiest, sunniest breakfast tea I have ever had. It warbled in perfect harmony with the oatmeal. It was like having breakfast across the table from Caruso and Melba singing love duets.

We explored Dublin on foot and by car, asking in vain for cock-a-leekie soup, which we had been led to believe was an Irish specialty. We got many puzzled looks, which is not surprising, since our guidebook had gotten it wrong: cock-a-leekie is a Scottish dish. What we found instead was pikelets.

Pikelets (rhymes with "bike-lets") aren't an Irish specialty, either. They are a kind of English yeast pancake that has apparently become a necessity of life for Dubliners, as it turns out that they are found in every convenience store. We first stumbled upon them one day during the off-hours when pubs and tea rooms are closed. Hunger had driven us to forage in a tiny dime store, and there they were, packets of them stacked up like books on a table and at room temperature. We bought two six-packs and a jar of jam. Each pikelet was six inches across and tantalizingly plump. Cold pancakes. Odd, we thought, yet somehow not unappealing. We returned to our car and used our fingers to spread jam on the new treats, which we rolled up and munched on while we drove around hunting for a street tea setup on the sidewalk.

Day-old pikelets are supposed to be eaten toasted and buttered and jammed, but eaten cold and unbuttered they have the same charm that cold

Ireland's per capita tea consumption is the highest in the world. It is said that the finest breakfast blends are found in Ireland, and Barry's of Cork makes the best "English" Breakfast tea I've ever had. You can write them at Barry's of Cork, Cork, Ireland. It'll get there.

At a street tea, mugs are laid out on a table or on an old door set on sawhorses, usually near a construction site. The sturdy white mugs are partly filled with milk poured in one grand gesture, the pitcher moving swiftly from row to row. Tea is added in the same fashion, and the whole scene is a generous and sociable sight to see.

Breakfast blends are most often made today with lots of African teas, often mixed with those from India and Ceylon. They can be dizzying combinations of up to twenty-five different teas, or, confusingly, made of one sturdy tea all by itself. They are always full-bodied, black, and high in caffeine.

The first breakfast tea so labeled was marketed over a hundred years ago, by a tea merchant named Drysdale on High Street in Edinburgh. The firm is still there today, and still content to call its innovation simply Breakfast Tea.

Temporary tea stations seem to follow people wherever they gather—at crossroads in the remote provinces of China and India, at cricket and rugby games, at picnics, at Wimbledon, in the gardens of stately homes, and even in the fields at harvest time. During World War II the railway stations in England offered the same service, using fancy rolling carts rather than trestle tables.

My pet breakfast tea theory is that the English, always imperious, stole the concept of an early-morning wake-me-up from the Scots, and claimed it as their own. The Irish, ever independent, changed the taste to a maltier and smokier version, calling it Irish Breakfast. Still later, the Germans up north in Ostfriesland fell into step with a breakfast tea of their own, but called it Ostfriesen tea, with no mention of breakfast at all. There they brew it very strong and sip it through layers of cream and sugar cubes held between their teeth. You can, too, for a taste of the Old World. Three cups before breakfast are not uncommon, clouded with unstirred cream. (This tea is so strong it can take cream instead of milk without being overwhelmed.) Then they go on drinking large pots of it all day. It's cold in northern Germany.

toast sometimes has when you are fidgeting by the stove in an abstracted moment and suddenly discover the goodness of it as is.

Round the cobblestoned streets we drove, holding a half-eaten pikelet in one hand, the map—or the steering wheel—in the other. I can hardly recall any moment when I so longed for a steaming mug, not only for my mouth and tummy but also for my sticky paw.

The church bells were ringing, the bikes were crisscrossing in and out in front of us. I prayed to the sweet Baby Jesus for tea. Suddenly, in the next block, a worker appeared and put up a barrier: Road Up. Construction. I got out, stepped around some loose pavement, legged it over a sandpile, and there like a scene in an MGM movie was our street tea.

The tea they were selling on the streets of Dublin undoubtedly came from one of the large tea companies that are referred to in the trade as "the big boys." Such tea is a mixture of Indian teas and short-leafed Ceylon teas, which means that it will be fast to infuse. For many people this *is* tea, the only kind they drink. Ask them what kind it is and they answer, "Oh, it's tea—just tea. Get it at the corner." The next step up in black teas is the tinned or boxed loose-leaf types put out by the major companies. Longer-leafed, they taste better (that is, more complex), and will remain that way for a longer time.

After we had done Dublin, we headed west and motored round the Ring of Kerry in our red VW convertible. The weather was sparkling and so were we, especially after acquiring brand-new bulky white Irish sweaters that bounced with light and bristled with energy. On the way to Kilkenny we chanced to meet on the road the saleslady who had sold us the sweaters the day before (whose name—Tess Mulready—we had remembered for some reason and would now never forget). She strode up to our open car and looked us over, in one sweeping motion, with the bluest eyes this side of Sweden. "Aye, you're *handsome,* now," she said in her throaty brogue, "that you are!" That was all, but it felt like the blessing we'd hoped to get from our parents. We drove off glowing. The world was bright, the sky was blue, the countryside was green, and the road was so inviting it might as well have been made of yellow brick.

That autumn southern Ireland was enjoying the sunniest, greenest, most *perfect* Saint Martin's summer anyone could remember. And we drove blissfully through it, likewise enjoying each other's charms, and assuming, in the innocence of youth, that everyone we met was delighted with us, too. Perhaps they were: I think we were the only tourists in the area that month, and indeed, everyone we encountered was earnest and honest and helpful and sweet. The memory of our parents' shocked disapproval had faded with Tess's words, and we were off.

The days were glorious beyond imagination. We had it all: the adventure of

For street tea and lunch counter teas, color predicts quality—the only time the color of brewed tea can be a signifier. Slightly gray, watered-down, milked-down, in-a-cracked-mug tea is to be avoided. When it's bad, one can be consoled with the phrase of a British gentleman friend: "Never mind; it's wet and warm, wet and warm. Drink up."

My first encounter with a street-tea scene was London, 1950, as Mother and I were touring the ruins around St. Paul's Cathedral. The reconstruction had begun, and there, in the midst of fireweed and rubble and the bottomless-looking holes in the ground, workers gathered at precisely four o'clock in the afternoon for tea.

One, a tiny, grimy, toothless fellow, complete with greasy cap, emerged from the earth, grinning, seated on the lower jaw of a huge earth-moving machine. He was carefully lowered to the sidewalk and set down like a precious teacup. He swaggered to the tea setup, took up his mug, turned, and raised it in salute to Mother, who stood nearby, looking very much the lady in her modest green traveling suit and tailored, beribboned hat.

each other and the adventure of the road; it was all new, driving on the left, meeting sometimes, to our astonishment, another car. The roads twisted about through almost deserted countryside where a modest cottage would occasionally appear round the bend, a trail of smoke connecting its thatched roof to the sky, a kerchiefed woman sitting motionless by the cottage door (or sometimes at the roadside, to relieve her solitude).

Our journey began to take on a storybook quality. When we arrived at small inns and pubs or knocked on the doors of guest cottages, we were sometimes greeted with stupefaction, as if we were apparitions of some kind, rather than merely novelties—just a couple of off-season Yankee tourists, after all. Then hospitality would reassert itself. We felt a little like knights errant, lost on a quest, humbly seeking food and shelter on our way. We stayed at some of these cottages, those that took overnight guests for a bit of extra income—very modest cottages, some of them, with no plumbing, dirt floors, smoky peat fires on the hearth, and straw mattresses slung on ropes lashed to rudely built bed frames. But we were as comfortable as if we had been guests at the Ritz.

We had only one slight complaint as we rambled through rural Ireland: afternoon tea was, invariably and maddeningly, precisely the same every day, no matter where we took it. Regardless of how many miles lay between Monday's tea and Tuesday's tea, the tea service looked eerily familiar. There were the three required kinds of tea sandwich—plain buttered bread, cucumber, and watercress—each buttered with the same stingy hand, cut into the same triangular crustless shape and size as yesterday's sandwiches, and even arranged in the same pattern on the plate. There were the two obligatory cakes: one a slice of pound cake, the other a slice of yellow commercial fruitcake studded with maraschino cherries and spiffily wrapped in cellophane. Every teatime was the perfect replica of the teatime before it. We began to fantasize that, hiding behind a screen, a leering gnome secretly watched us inhale our tea every after-

High" and "low" are often misused when applied to tea. High tea (or "meat tea," or "knife-and-fork tea") is a simple but substantial middle-class supper. Low tea is afternoon tea. Some think these terms derive from the height of the menu card: a low tea has a short menu, a high tea a long one. The afternoon tea now served in hotel lobbies and fancy tea rooms is often described, wrongly, as high tea, probably because "high tea" sounds more highfalutin. Another etymology is that the terms refer to the height of the table: afternoon tea is served in the home by a hostess at a conveniently low table in the parlor, while the supper table is at the normal height for the comfortable consumption of a meal with knife and fork.

noon, rubbing his awful little hands together, then packed up his cooking gear and scurried ahead of us to our next stop in time to prepare us the insanely identical repast.

At noon we always picnicked. One day, no grocer's having presented itself that morning, we picnicked badly, eking out an unsatisfying lunch from a couple of bruised and overripe bananas, rubbery cheese, and day-old bread. Then we posed for snapshots of each other leaning against a stone wall, with massive, silver-lined clouds in the background and blue heather in the foreground. We didn't have a camera, actually, having decided to travel without the fuss and paraphernalia and rely on our memories. Still, we posed; and sure enough, I still have the pictures.

An hour later it had turned colder, and the open car let in the damp. The terrain became desolate, with fewer and fewer dwellings alongside the deserted road. As it got later, we began to get tired, and very hungry. Our minds and stomachs were ready for tea, and we even began hoping that our gnome was waiting around the next bend. We rehearsed how we would say, rather casually, without sounding desperate, "Oh, and a double order of sandwiches, please." (One did not want to play the greedy American.) But we did not pass a single bed-and-breakfast home, let alone a hotel or tea room. The rare cottages we saw had tile roofs and propane tanks—sure signs that the occupants were just prosperous enough to take offense should strangers ask for a meal or an overnight room for a few shillings.

Then, just as we began to despair, on a hilltop ahead we spied a large, comfortable-looking house, and at the bottom of the hill, a gas pump, with a sign. A hotel? A school? Or only a gas pump? We pulled in, reassured by a hand-lettered sign hung on a line between two trees: Sound Your Hooter for Service. We hooted. From the house up the hill a tall, snaggle-toothed woman came wobbling swiftly down. She was wearing a shawl over a sweater with crusty elbows, an apron over an old skirt, over another apron and an older skirt, over leggings, over socks. Her hair was a tangle of gray and brown, her nose was long, but her face healthy. We had apparently interrupted her from some compelling task at the house above. She pumped the gas peremptorily. We hesitated. A closer look at the house and our hearts sank; it was obviously a private home. Dare we ask? Hunger decided it. I plunged in: We were hungry; could she provide us with, perhaps . . . an egg? I waited respectfully. Hand on hip, she turned toward the house, then back to us, and muttered, "Aye yes. We-elll . . ."

"Oh, *good!*" I responded forcefully, ". . . and perhaps some bread and butter?" You could have smelled our hunger. She assessed the situation. This was surely inconvenient, but it might mean a little profit. "Aye well then, why don't I just *do* you a tea?" (Yes! Why not!) She started up the hill. "The muffins, they're old now," she said, almost to herself. She never smiled. We trailed after her.

The door to the old house swung open and we smelled dogs and cats, old cabbage, old wood, and new linoleum. Everything was clean, but just barely. It felt as if no one actually *lived* in the house; its occupants slept there, but life was outside. It was very cold inside. Our hostess opened the door to a small parlor. We stepped in, and she switched on the heater and left. We sat down on kitchen chairs with padded seat cushions of black and orange chintz in a little doggie pattern. The room was stuffed with old newspapers, farm magazines, dying potted plants, and sleeping cats. Afraid she might hear us, we said nothing as our eyes wandered over the badly lit room. The sky outside darkened, and as it began to warm up ever so slightly inside, we sat silent in our chairs, afraid that any mishap now might cost us our supper.

The tea arrived first, shrouded in an intensely orange tea cozy decorated with a pink cat's face. She set down the tray on the tiled central table and exited, puffing. We fell on it and unveiled the large brown teapot. On the tray beside it were a metal pot of hot water, a pitcher of thick rich whole milk, and a huge, high-sided bowl that held at least two pounds of sugar, with a large soup spoon stuck upright in the middle. This was a serious sugar bowl. It matched no other dish. Its look bespoke decades of use in a household where sugar was consumed lavishly.

Reverently and somewhat shakily we poured the tea. It was malty and rich and a bit muddy, as if it had been made in a hurry. There was no hint of smokiness, but it still had depth and an expansive allure about it that was almost seductive. I suspect we were just famished, but I remember it as being two or three cuts above hotel and bed-and-breakfast teas, and I've never tasted its equal.

In and out trundled the mistress of this household, like a tea cart with a loose caster. I visualized the pantry gradually being emptied of everything it held. In came a fresh slab of butter with the marks of the butter paddle still on it, a dollop that had been scooped onto the plate with what my mother used to call "a big hand." The slab probably weighed a pound or more, and this harbinger of real farm cooking perked me up considerably. Then came the bread ("whole meal," as they call it in the British Isles, whole wheat to us), thick and soft and chewy, with that lovely crunchy crust. I will never forget the taste of that bread. Fast followed a hunk of ham—not too fat, not too lean—and a plate of sliced tomatoes, obviously from the garden, with absolutely nothing on them. We consumed in silence. Next we were presented with eggs in egg cups accompanied by two tiny spoons carved from bone. (After that day, I started looking for little bone spoons in every antique shop we came upon.) More bread, more butter. An almost symphonic momentum was building. The muffins came in, and although they may have been a day old, the crumb was so fine and the taste so nutty (despite their actual nutlessness) that all was forgiven. A scattering of boughten biscuits appeared (arrowroot cookies, we'd call them), and then, with a big *whump!* an oversized wedge of Swiss cheese was set down before us, so perfect it might have come straight out of a Tom and Jerry cartoon. An afterthought, we decided later. I imagined her husband in the kitchen grousing at her: "Are you giving them *everything* now?"

Then the pace and the mood shifted. A new movement was beginning. A section of pound cake appeared, all alone on a plain white plate. This was a cousin of the hotel pound cake we had been served every day, everywhere else, but the texture and the crumb were a little heartier and the taste a little richer. Still without uttering a word, our hostess presented us with two bowls of vanilla ice cream, the kind with black dots of vanilla bean in it. (By now, we were scarcely registering her entrances and exits; all our attention was on the dazzling succession of offerings.)

Immediately following the ice cream came The Cake. I had been expecting it. I sensed that having hauled herself up for the occasion, she was going to pull out all the stops, and that would surely mean a climactic second cake. But The Cake itself was a terrific disappointment to look at. It, too, must have been left over from yesterday or the day before. About a third had already been cut away. It sagged badly. The only word to describe it was *lurid,* but we decided to call it the Horrid Cake. The layers were a hysterical, psychedelic fuchsia; its thick white frosting was white, *too* white; it looked as if it would glow in the dark. Garish gumdrops studded the remaining two-thirds of the sagging hulk.

We paused, apprehensively. This had to be our hostess's last offering. The occasion had demanded a second cake; and she'd delivered it. (I recalled Truman Capote's boast about a childhood Sunday dinner when company came: "We had *two* kinds of cake and tutti-frutti ice cream *from the drug store!*" This Southern tradition must have come from the British Isles, where company teas, even nursery teas, seem to require two cakes.) Perhaps it was our surroundings or the fact that we had been so hungry, but I really don't think so. No, the Horrid Cake was actually quite tasty: eggy, light, and not too sweet. Hideous, yes, but perfectly delightful to eat. Perhaps the food-coloring bottle had slipped in her hand. And even the gumdrops provided a welcome little sugar punch. I dreamt of future children's birthday parties, knowing that I would try to bake such a cake.

We started to pull ourselves together to go, but the door creaked open and our hostess made one more entrance, this time with the hint of a smile on her face. In her hands she carried a tray with four steaming tarts, fresh out of the oven. Two were apple; the other two, rhubarb. For some reason, I would never have connected rhubarb with Ireland, but there it was. It had been easy as pie for her to make pastry dough and roll out and bake these tarts, even while she was occupied with serving all that had preceded them.

We poured and ate, and purred with satisfaction. What we couldn't eat I wrapped in orange paper napkins and stuffed in my purse. She had certainly made good her promise to "do us a tea." And this had been, of course, a high tea, a full-fledged, authentic, knife-and-fork tea—actually, a knife-and-fork-and-several-kinds-of-spoon tea. We got out our money and waited. After a bit, our mistress returned, hands on hips, and without smiling, tossing her head back ever so slightly, asked us, "D'you think ye can manage on that, then?" We nodded and murmured our thanks and asked for the bill. We knew it was time to go; the curtain had rung down. There was no mention of staying overnight and we knew it would have been rude for us to have hinted at it—or even to ask if she knew of a place. She reached into her pocket and pulled out a bill inscribed in a beautiful hand: the grand total was ten shillings, about a dollar forty in American money at the time, about five dollars today. We mumbled our thanks, paid, and moved out the door. Gray twilight greeted us, and the damp. But our hearts and stomachs were so fortified that we were fearless. The job of finding a place to stay in the dark would be a lark.

I think that was the afternoon that wedded me to tea as assuredly as I was wedded to my mate. Tea in my youth had been liberating, a path to self-confidence. The notion that I could achieve had softly crept into my consciousness as I smiled and snuggled into bed after the wonderful Faculty Follies tea. This experience was altogether different. This tea had given me not just self-esteem, but courage. (Tea still makes me brave: a stout mug of good, strong black tea and I feel ready to face the most difficult phone call.) A famous remark by Elizabeth I came to mind: "I may be a woman, but I have the heart and stomach of a king!" I held my head high as I lowered myself into the car and closed the door. I had two serious and lifetime loves now—my own sweetheart—and tea.

RECIPES

Pikelets

MAKES 18 PIKELETS

Pikelets are best when someone is at the stove making them for you and you can tuck into them right away as they come off the griddle. However, if you're the cook and you want to sit down and eat with everyone else, the pikelets will hold rather nicely stacked between paper towels and kept warm in the oven. I like the batter rather thick, in the Irish style, but they are still delicious when the batter is thinned out with warm water or milk. Serve with plenty of butter and an assertive jam.

1 teaspoon dry yeast	2 tablespoons vegetable oil
1 teaspoon sugar	⅔ cup warm water
2½ cups warm milk	Butter
1 tablespoon salt	
3 cups unbleached all-purpose flour	

In a large bowl, stir the yeast and sugar into ½ cup of the warm milk and let stand for 5 to 10 minutes. Stir in the salt and the rest of the milk, and beat in the flour with a wooden spoon. Cover and let rise 1½ hours at room temperature. Stir in the oil and as much of the warm water as it takes to make the batter thin enough for pancakes.

Heat a griddle or a large heavy skillet over medium heat and grease with a little butter. When it sizzles, spoon or pour out a generous amount of batter onto the griddle or into the skillet, about ⅓ cup per pikelet. A pikelet should be at least 4 inches in diameter, so you may wish to make them one at a time. Cook until the top is shiny with big bubbles in it and brown around the edges. Flip

the pikelet and cook the other side. When it is done, put it on a warm plate, and either serve it right away or cover with a paper towel and slip it inside a moderate oven to keep warm. Wipe the skillet or griddle clean, grease with a little more butter, and keep turning out the pikelets.

Irish Country Bread (Barm Brack)

This recipe is by Monica Spiller, a Bay Area baker who specializes in re-creating the traditional breads of the British Isles. I described my Irish whole meal bread memories to her and she baked this bread for me that tastes almost exactly like the unforgettable loaf we were served at our gas station tea. It's leavened with a natural starter and speckled with whole malted wheat flakes, hence the name "Barm Brack." ("Barm" is the old British word for leavening, and "brack" means speckled.) Obtain, from a bread-making friend, 1 cup of mild bread dough starter. (A mild sourdough would be fine.)

For 1 loaf (about 1 pound):

1 cup refreshed whole wheat
   bread starter or barm (see
   page 50 for method)
½ cup malted wheat flakes
   (dark roasted)
⅓ cup water (for soaking the
   malted wheat flakes)

1 tablespoon barley malt
   extract (syrup)
1¼ cups whole wheat flour
½ teaspoon salt
1 tablespoon water

A few days before baking: Begin refreshing the whole wheat starter as explained on page 50. The starter used in the dough should have been refreshed 6 to 12 hours previously.

Twenty-four hours before baking: In a bowl, mix the malted wheat flakes with the water for soaking. Cover the bowl and leave at cool room temperature for 12 to 24 hours; all the water will be absorbed by the wheat.

On baking day: Place the starter in a mixing bowl, followed by the soaked wheat flakes, barley malt extract, and whole wheat flour. In a small bowl, dissolve the salt in the water and add to the mixing bowl. Mix all ingredients until just blended. Cover the mixing bowl and leave the dough to rise at warm room temperature (86°F), until it has risen to about 1½ times its original volume (1 to 3 hours).

Knead the dough to complete the mixing and to develop the dough until it can be stretched into a paper-thin sheet (5 to 20 minutes). With water-moistened hands, form the dough into a ball and place on a dampened wooden board. Cover with an inverted bowl, and leave to rest 20 to 40 minutes at warm room temperature.

Prepare a covered ceramic bread baker by generously sprinkling whole wheat flour onto the base, to prevent sticking.

Reshape the dough into a ball. Lightly coat it with whole wheat flour and place in the base of the ceramic bread baker. Cover with the ceramic lid and let rise in a warm room until nearly fully risen (30 to 45 minutes), or nearly doubled in size.

Preheat the oven to 425°F.

Just before baking, score the loaf with a cross, and replace the ceramic lid. Bake covered for 25 minutes, then remove the lid. Bake for another 5 to 15 minutes, until well browned and firm to the touch.

Allow to cool completely, on a wooden rack, before eating.

To make a refreshed Whole Wheat Bread Starter, or Barm

MAKES 2 CUPS REFRESHED STARTER

Choose a starter that is a vigorous leavener and mild in flavor, such as a sourdough starter, one that can be maintained with whole wheat flour supplemented with a little malted flour and water.

> 1 cup starter (at least 12 hours old)
> ⅔ cup whole wheat flour
> ½ teaspoon malted wheat flour
> ⅔ cup water

Refresh the starter with whole wheat flour, malted wheat flour, and water, using the proportions given above. Keep the refreshed starter loosely covered at 55° to 60°F, and repeat the refreshment 2 or 3 times at 12-hour intervals.

From 6 to 12 hours after the last refreshment, the starter will be ready to use to make bread on baking day.

Horrid Cake

MAKES ONE 8- OR 9-INCH 2-LAYER CAKE

Horrid Cake is easy to make and very tasty. Kids take to it since it looks like a child's drawing of the ideal birthday cake. Any three- or four-egg yellow or white cake recipe will do; I use this one-bowl version, adapted from the Hurry-Up Cake in The Joy of Cooking, *but I reduce the sugar because the gumdrops pack such a wallop. You will get the best results if all the ingredients are at room temperature.*

Be lavish with the frosting and decorate freely, using the most garish combination of gumdrops at your disposal.

3½ cups cake flour

2 cups less 2 tablespoons sugar

1 cup soft butter

4 eggs (room temperature)

1 teaspoon salt

3½ teaspoons baking powder

2 teaspoons vanilla

1 teaspoon red food coloring

1 recipe Royal Icing (see
   page 52)

One 13-ounce package
   gumdrops

Heat the oven to 350°F. Grease 2 round cake pans, 8 or 9 inches in diameter. (I prefer 8-inch.) Sift the cake flour before you measure it, and resift with the sugar into a large bowl. Add the butter, eggs, salt, baking powder, vanilla, and food coloring. Beat with a whisk, electric mixer, or any old how for 2 or 3 minutes. Divide the batter into the 2 greased pans and bake in the preheated oven for 35 to 40 minutes. Cool, frost with the Royal Icing, and decorate with the gumdrops, making it as splendiferous as possible.

Royal Icing

MAKES ABOUT 2 CUPS

The glycerin keeps the icing from overhardening.

> 2 egg whites
> 3 cups confectioners' sugar
> 1 tablespoon lemon juice
> ¼ teaspoon salt
> 1 or 2 drops glycerin (available at drugstores)

Put the egg whites, sugar, lemon juice, salt, and glycerin in a mixing bowl. Beat vigorously until soft peaks emerge from the mixture.

Chapter Four

THE BIG BACKYARD TEA-IN AND OTHER TEA PARTIES

It was April 1972. I sat wedged in the corner of a low-slung, cushy couch in a well-appointed home in the Berkeley hills. With one hand I was balancing on my knee a Limoges plate on which rested a slice of lemon tart; with the other I was tugging at my skirt, an Yves St. Laurent knockoff. As I wriggled I could feel every miserable inch of my girdle. Somehow the heavy wool skirt was prickling me all the way through its lining underneath, and through my nylon slip, my hose, and the accursed girdle itself.

In front of me yawned the awkward open space between couch and the coffee table where my teacup was resting, a space more than wide enough to accommodate my long legs and what my husband calls, lovingly, my sturdy thighs. Everything about my position seemed too low, too soft, or too far away. To reach for the cup required a major squirm forward, then a tug at my skirt, then more sliding to the edge of the couch. Then the long reach across the abyss and the motions had to be reversed: a backward shimmy, and with every shift of a few inches, a tug at the skirt plus a tug at the sleeveless overblouse, which was riding

up my back. (These YSL outfits were made for Jackie Kennedy types to wear posed before an eighteenth-century spinet.)

Once again I was quietly furious. My circle of friends had begun another round of Julia Child–inspired dinner parties; an unacknowledged competition was on, and next week it was my turn. I sighed. That meant three full days of exhaustion: two to get ready and one to recover. What would I cook? I could hardly think because nearby a group of male academics were relentlessly and loudly boring a hole right into the center of my head with posturing political polemic. With every ounce of my ample being, I wished that they would button up. Why weren't they concerning themselves with what was obviously the only important subject at this dinner party: Why was the lemon tart so delicious? And how did that crust get so tender? *My* crust was always stiff and tasteless.

My legs ached to move. And to make matters worse, my mind turned to what I had learned that afternoon: The night before, there had been a delicious scandal at our new little neighborhood French restaurant, called (unpronounceably) Chez Panisse. A group of diners had become so intoxicated by the food and wine that in a burst of Dionysian inspiration they had disappeared into the bathrooms upstairs, emerged stark naked, and streaked through the place—at the peak of the dinner service!—whereupon everyone had applauded and toasted the daring dashers with Champagne. The bacchanal had continued. Joined by friends who worked at the restaurant, the streakers had circled the block au naturel, come back to get their clothes, and adjourned to a nearby apartment, where they ate up leftovers from Panisse and drank more Champagne. Then at dawn they had driven off to the beach for more frolic. It was too much to think about: the long hair (of both sexes) blowing in the wind, the bare feet in the sand, the women in billowing caftans with no brassieres. The freedom! The fun!

Sick with envy, I reached for another piece of lemon tart. As my upper arm strained against the armhole of my overblouse, I could feel the flesh reddening and chafing. I felt like I was being cut. Suddenly I had a dizzying memory: I was interviewing Miss Hickenhauser, my veteran spinster social studies teacher, for our high school paper. "What is *really* important in life, Miss Hickenhauser?" She squinted, grinned, and barked out two words: "Lemon pie!" It had been so unlike her. Now, when I was reaching for more lemon tart, her pronouncement came rushing back to me. With that reach, I realized I was at a watershed. Why be *punished* in the pursuit of pleasure? It was time for rebellion, time to cast off clothes that pinched and restrained, time to turn away from the Ping-Pong of intellectual talk that went nowhere and ignored the luscious stuff of life. It was time to perfect my *own,* ever more delicious, lemon tarts. From that moment, at the apex of my vexation with respectable middle age, lemon tart became forever and inextricably associated with the birth of my new life as a full-blown, over-forty, middle-class faux hippie.

One of my first acts of rebellion was the anti-dinner-party. The guests were greeted by my youngest and prettiest baby-sitter dressed in a black smock and a white apron, her long blond hair plaited in coils around her ears. She was our decoy to throw the guests off balance. Could it be that the Gustafsons had hired a maid? In the living room the guests' confusion grew as they were offered processed cheese on colored toothpicks, and canned concocted cocktails. Once seated around the table, resplendent with our best silver and Portuguese linen, their perplexity turned to horror and finally hilarity as the maid served canned tomato soup, canned spaghetti, frozen Salisbury steaks, and frozen spinach souf-flé. The only real food was good bread, and there was enough of it, along with good Champagne being poured out with a generous hand, that when the wine took over, the guests forgave the atrocious food and my little joke, and got so much into the spirit of the thing that when the pièce de résistance appeared—reconstituted packaged butterscotch pudding—they even ate some of it, and sighed nostalgically for the cuisine of the fifties.

Still hungry of course, we repaired to the kitchen, where we took pictures of the mess of empty boxes and cans, and ate more good baguettes and some decent cheese and drank more Champagne, until we were all roaming around the house, dancing, and letting down our hair. How wonderful we were, and how clever to be free to do what we pleased! No grown-ups here! No rules! Those among us who were "into TM" (Transcendental Meditation) even revealed our secret mantras. It was all a wild success, a party that is still talked about over twenty years later.

That blowout turned our passion for good food right-side-up. Our parties became more frequent and more spontaneous, but we went back to caring passionately and seriously about food. We still cooked to impress one another, but as we expanded our repertoires the style of our hospitality relaxed. We began giving parties on just a day or two's notice. All any of us had to do was buy two cases of Champagne, clear off the dining room table, and stand back. About eight o'clock our friends would begin to arrive with masterpiece after masterpiece for the table, everyone charged up with the excitement of "the food thing" and eager to show off some culinary inventiveness. The music was loud and the dancing was free.

No one, however, had hosted a big afternoon garden tea party, so I stepped boldly into the breach. For this affair, instead of trusting to spontaneous party combustion, I sent out invitations, adding that hat and gloves would be obligatory. I was stunned by the reaction: *What do you* mean, *hats! I don't own one! Is this dinner, or formal, or what? What* is *a tea party, anyway?* I should have known; in California, traditions are few, and not everyone's childhood had been filled with romping good times around the tea table.

Okay, it would be not just a whoop, but a spoof: the scene's first-ever Tea-in. Don't have a hat? Rent one at the door, for twenty-five cents a pop. (A friend donated the Easter hats created by her art class for adults with Down's syndrome: wonderful free-spirited polyester-felt creations in psychedelic shades.) Glove rental was at the bargain rate of a dime a pair for dress gloves; garden gloves were free.

The menu was strictly traditional: cucumber sandwiches (two kinds), Dorothy's jam sponge cake (sure to please), my own trifle (built three days in advance to allow the flavors to mingle), and various boughten biscuits (the arrowroot cracker kind), just to be on the safe side. For the tea itself, I wanted the latest faddish fruit-flavored tea, black currant, but it was stocked only in tea bags. Just before the party began, ashamed to be caught serving bagged tea, I feverishly scissored them open and dumped the tiny bits into warm tea pots, ready to go.

The passion for flavored tea is age-old. Jasmine tea existed for hundreds of years before bergamot-scented Earl Grey appeared. Samuel Johnson dried strips of orange peel on his windowsill and dunked them into his tea as a purge. I like to think this historical tidbit inspired Ruth Bigelow to add dried orange peel to her new tea blend in 1944. The scene opens: "But Ruth," her husband remarks, "people will be constantly commenting on that." Exactly. Constant Comment is still terribly popular with the L.O.L.'s (Little Old Ladies) and many others.

Beware: Tea will take on the flavor of anything left in or near it. A tea tin you use to store an electrical cord will, if you go back to using it for leaves, bring forth Electrical Cord Tea. Russian Caravan is a paramount example. Tea for the czars went by caravan from China across central Asia to Saint Petersburg; the trip took a year, and at the end of its journey the tea tasted exactly like what it had been close to: smoky campfires, sweaty camels and men, and the insides of leather saddlebags. The last camel left Canton in 1900, but our Russian Caravan carries on, smoked and flavored as exotically as possible.

Guests mounted the steps and peered through the hallway into the dining room. I asked them to choose their own teacup from among the dozens of matched and mismatched ones on the table. Here I used to advantage the training in Advanced Teasing I received from my big brother: "Don't be afraid, this is just a little intelligence and character test! No one is watching. You can do it. There! A beautiful cup, and a perfect match for your orange tennis shoes." It worked; soon everyone was out in the garden laughing and comparing outfits. And outfits there were: late-hippie dishabille (my foodie pals); a three-piece suit (my doctor); a white nun's habit, complete with wimple (Sister Allyn, the principal of our kids' school); Southampton khakis and white canvas hat, driving gloves stuck in breast pocket (the economics professor from across the street). My strategy was to mix 'em up and see what happened.

My baking buddy Dorothy had come with her signature jam sponge cake, the one her mom used to bake. She circulated around the lawn, her cake plate held high in one hand, a knife in the other, serving slices. She looked like a Dispensing Angel. Dorothy is round, the cake was round, and her motions were round. Anyone over forty who tasted her cake had to blink back tears of happiness and thank her for bringing alive sweet memories of youth.

My trifle made a sensation of a different kind. Men became wickedly interested in it after realizing it was full of alcohol. (Alcoholic or not, constructed dishes—ones built up of layers and assembled, rather than simply "cooked"— seem to have a powerful hold on men, no doubt related to the impulse that leads to Lego toys and Erector sets.) The trifle rose to new heights when one of the guests, an ordinarily restrained Englishwoman dressed in what might be called "regulation lady" (straight, knee-length skirt; prim blouse; sensible pumps; and "an interesting little necklace that Jeffrey brought me from India"), took one bite, and, hoisting the huge bowl over her head, shouted with uncharacteristic abandon, "This is the best trifle I have ever had in the whole of my life!"

The cucumber sandwiches didn't play so badly either. One kind had been Rutabaga's specialty when we were growing up. Every summer at the lake she would make luscious cucumber sandwiches: good white bread with the crusts on, thick slices of cucumber, and a thick layer of butter and store-bought mayonnaise. Sometimes she salted the cucumbers, and sometimes not; it depended on her mood. After working on our jigsaw puzzle in the screened porch, we would take along a whole sackful to eat down by the lake, dangling our feet in the cool water. The birch trees overhead were green and white, soft and leafy. The sandwiches were green and white, too, and crisp and squishy at the same time. (Of course we were too young to understand more than vaguely just how lovely all this was.) The other kind was the coolly elegant English cucumber sandwich we found in books: paper-thin slices of peeled cucumber layered between thin slices of heavily buttered dense white bread, trimmed crustless and cut into perfect ivory-piano-key shapes. We found that the secret is to spread the sweet butter evenly right to the very edge of the bread and salt the cukes ever so delicately.

The Tea-in menu deserved more than just the one "tea" (the rosy-hued black currant), but not until the end of the party did I produce it: it was pink, too—pink Champagne, cleverly hidden in ice tubs behind the washing machine in the basement. About six o'clock, as the party started to wane, I rushed down and started decanting the bubbly into teapots. Then, with the help of six friends, we served it super-blitzkrieg-style. A panzer division couldn't have done it better. The troops fanned out in every direction, zapping every little group of lazy-afternoon guests, scoring a direct hit on teacup after teacup. By that time, many guests were so overcome by the excessive high spirits of the occasion, the sugar, and the combination of people, that they failed to identify what, exactly, was being poured into their cups, and asked me—seriously!—where *this* tea had come

from. "Certainly an unusual tea," they murmured, swaying and hanging on to the nearest tree. Many left about dusk, but a core group stayed on until two in the morning, singing Fred Astaire songs and eating leftover cucumber sandwiches in the kitchen. Occasionally one of them tried to be Astaire, and would attempt an effortless-looking fox-trot glide, holding his cup aloft and smiling a sideways, sophisticated-in-spite-of-himself smile. My only regret was that Rutabaga lived too far away to attend; she would have approved of the cucumber sandwiches.

As the decades gradually passed, so did that exuberant mood that was always urging us on to make another fabulous meal, right now, today, tonight! And a good thing, because giving a dinner party, no matter how impromptu, still took its toll on me. So I reverted to doing what I knew how to do best, while having fun at the same time: I started giving frequent tea parties—real tea parties, but small ones. At such a tea party, all is civility and fun. There are no danger spots except the deadly lull in conversation, and that can always be, if not entirely avoided, at least neutralized by a non sequitur, preferably delivered with one eye crossed. A stunner, this stratagem has never failed me.

Organizing food for a tea party is infinitely simpler than trying to plan and execute a dinner party menu. I stick to the clear-off-the-table spirit of the seventies, make one spectacular treat of my own, then ask each guest to bring a homemade tea goodie, or a favorite bakery one. My energy goes into planning a good mix of guests, and setting my table with the right china. Chips and cracks and scrambled styles don't matter. If it's a pretty piece I like, inherited or acquired, on it goes. Even housekeeping is easy. I have taken to heart the advice of Mrs. Genevieve Bade of the Faculty Women's Club: "Always remember the Two T's!" she would cry, "toilet and telephone! Both must be clean." Most guests, she assured me, do not look for the dust under the table; but things they might use must be pristine.

I confess that when I started giving frequent small tea parties I fancied myself as a latter-day Mrs. Hester Thrale, the hostess of the small salon where Dr.

Samuel Johnson and his circle talked brilliantly in eighteenth-century London. Our dining room is the perfect size to encourage talking, but I didn't find my own Dr. Johnson until I met Dr. Sterling Bunnell.

He was a regular lunch patron at Chez Panisse when I began working there as a hostess. He displayed an intense, uncensored curiosity about, and appreciation of, all matters culinary, asking questions that revealed an astonishing breadth of knowledge—anthropological, historical, psychological, biological. A great unkempt bear of a man, he was also remarkable for his startlingly unselfconscious disregard for the usual conventions of dress. New employees were inevitably taken aback: "Who is that man?" they would whisper to me after he was seated at his usual table. They quickly grew used to his eccentricities. His arrival would be the occasion for fond glee among the staff when he turned up with his shirt making a vague connection with his pants for once. Good news travels fast. "Socks today," someone would announce. A pause and another look. "And they match!"

One day, about to pay his bill, he discovered he'd lost his wallet. Wild-eyed, he searched everywhere, lifting glassware and napkin, peering under the table, repeatedly slapping his chest and searching his pockets. As he was leaving, apologetic and still distraught, I spotted the wallet as he started down the stairs to the street. It was dangling somewhere in the neighborhood behind his right knee, swinging loosely, attached only to a thread from a torn and turned-out rear pocket. I pointed it out. He retrieved it, swung his big head around, looked at me piercingly, and exclaimed, "You're a genius!" Recognition at last. It was his assessment of me that ultimately qualified him for the role of the great Dr. Johnson.

Asked his name, he volunteers "Sterling," never "Dr. Bunnell." But he is an M.D., a psychiatrist, a desert naturalist, and a consultant to the University of California and all the arts colleges in the Bay Area. He is also a poet, a falconer, and the father of five. My favorite Sterling sighting is a side view: standing sockless and solitary in a light drizzle, his hooded falcon perched immobile on his gauntleted forearm, his gravely classical profile framed by his slouch hat and his grizzled uncombed curls, watching intently as his young son plays football.

The first time he came to one of my tea parties he inspected our house much as a curious eight-year-old unaccompanied by his mother might do. He peered everywhere, pulling up and letting down the shades, and perusing the views; he examined the furniture and tried it out; and he studied the contents of cupboards and sideboards. Mrs. Bade might have disapproved, but I was delighted. Isn't this what we all would like to do, but don't dare? And as I had guessed, he was a dynamo of conversation.

With Sterling at the table, the topic might segue in an instant from the edibility of gastropods to the Peloponnesian War to how the magnetic fields around certain protein molecules look exactly like the whorls of wind-eroded desert sandstone. When I have to go to the kitchen, I may completely miss the transition. Once I returned to the dining room to hear Sterling proclaim magisterially, "Besides, I find that ghouls do very well on a low-protein diet." There was a roar of laughter.

Time almost seems to slow down around the tea table in the balmy days of spring and early fall, when the quiet charm of another era seeps into our dining room. The street outside is quiet and we can hear the distant bells of the campanile on the university campus. The old-fashioned yellow wallpaper makes the afternoon light streaming through the bay-view window all the mellower, and in the very late afternoon, when the light turns a melon pink and the conversation calms down from its early exuberance to the hush of shared confidences, it truly feels as if we are suspended in our own golden shell, living life as it should be lived.

One harassed businessman I know told me that he would cancel any appointment for the chance to come to tea. For him it is a time of complete escape. He is old enough to remember Berkeley in the days when the music that floated out of students' open windows through the cypress and the pines was all acoustic, and the air was filled with the sounds of bird song and distant pianos and guitars instead of traffic and heavy metal. "Your tea parties are like that," he told me once, "like taking a vacation in the quiet past."

One especially memorable afternoon I invited an all-star cast: luminaries in disparate fields who fit together perfectly. In order of appearance, the group consisted of the Bay Area's most distinguished writer on wine, a transplanted Englishman, the sort who gives good manners a good name; an eloquent lady linguist from the university; a celebrated Chinese businesswoman, a retired restaurateur with beautiful aristocratic posture and a Mandarin accent; an investigative journalist, a confident and bold-spirited woman who always looks snappy and stylish; a well-spoken and elegant Englishwoman, a retired diplomat whose musical accent has wonderful slushy sibilants; Sterling, of course; and me, as the maid.

I don't believe I could ever find a more reliable and sensitive maid than myself. Besides, much as I enjoy playing the grande dame, I don't think I could ever get used to tinkling a little silver bell to alert a uniformed kitchen maid. (Looking back at my youth in the Faculty Grove, I now understand the appeal of that little light switch on the dining room floor that I thought so ridiculous.)

My all-star tea party began with the choosing of the teacups, always a successful ploy. Conversation began with the gratifying flattery of the linguist, who gestured languidly around her; how she loved our dining room filled with quiet, amplitude, and refinement. The journalist leaned across the table, all elbows, whisked up an egg salad sandwich, and asked Sterling what he did. Of course, that was a little complicated to summarize, and soon Sterling had stood up abstractedly and was discoursing about desert flora, microbiology, and archaeology. He picked up Aunt Vertie's filigreed blue Venetian glass bowl with one hand, raised his teacup with the other,

and continued his discourse. I held my breath. The Chinese lady remarked on the bowl, which somehow prompted the Englishwoman to describe a garden in Cornwall. Sterling set down the bowl, and I excused myself to put on the kettle.

From the kitchen I could hear the talk veer off into an opinionated exchange about the funeral of Alexander the Great. I prepared three pots of tea: Yunnan, Earl Grey, and my best Darjeeling of the moment, from the Lingia garden. I returned with the first pot and began my spiel about my beloved Yunnan tea, but I cut it short when I saw the guests spy the Meyer lemon tarts on the sideboard. Egg salad sandwiches might be an everyday tea party treat, but not my tarts. They are the only thing I have ever made that has drawn the accolade "fantastic" from Alice Waters. And fantastic they are. Meyer lemon trees thrive in Berkeley; they bear juicy fruit with an entirely distinctive sweetness. Our tree—a bush, really—is just outside our bedroom window. Asking a child to fetch a lemon means a sudden retreat to the bedroom—and puzzled looks from the guest.

Darjeelings are the mindblowers of the tea world. Mike Spillane, the West Coast tea broker, said it best: "The harder it is to explain what it tastes like, the better your Darjeeling is."

Like vineyards, Darjeeling gardens are chancy and definitely have good and bad years. Even leaves from the same garden and the same year will express themselves differently each time you drink them. Like visits to a friend, each encounter is different and unrepeatable, although your friend is always the same person. Darjeelings are often used to perk up blends. Experiment at home; try mixing a Keemun that's winy and mellow with a Darjeeling for sparkle and zip.

The names of some major gardens are Margaret's Hope, Goomtee, Runglee, Rungliot, Thurbo, Balasun, Jungpana, Makabari, Castleton, Lingia, and Selimbong. If you get a chance, buy a quarter-pound, or take some to your hostess. Ten dollars will buy a lot of heaven.

The look of the dry leaf of a good Darjeeling should be clean; that is, it shouldn't have many incomplete, raggedy, or squirrelly-looking leaves. It should have the look of a finished, uniform product. It should look expensive.

> *The finest Darjeelings are demanding and must be steeped with care. I have it on good authority that Elizabeth II drinks Darjeeling every day—religiously timed to steep exactly five minutes—and so does her mum, and so did both her grandmums. In general, however, Darjeelings are best steeped three to four minutes, although one Darjeeling that is perfectly balanced after three and a half minutes may be undrinkably astringent after four, while another may be steeped for as long as seven or eight minutes.*
>
> *Though the queen may do so, do not subject your fine Darjeeling to a silver pot. A china pot is far preferable.*
>
> *Darjeelings do not require milk. I have known, however, a few otherwise perfectly reasonable people who do add it. One doesn't mess with fine Champagne and one doesn't mess with fine Darjeeling. Besides, it turns the tea a nasty gray sludgy color and ruins the fresh sparkle and interplay of the flavors.*
>
> *No lemon either.*

I delivered the remaining two teapots and boasted about my lemon tarts and the summer pudding that would follow. Then I poured, muffled the pots in tea cozies for the duration, and passed the tarts. We attacked them. Compliments wafted pleasantly about my ears, as the guests marveled at the thin, sweet lemon slices embedded in the custard. I drank Earl Grey with my dessert, to complement the lemony flavor of the tart with the citrus echo in the bergamot-flavored tea. The English wine connoisseur's choice was Darjeeling, of course.

The conversation soared, led by Sterling's unexpected lateral flights of erudition. By and by, I remembered the pudding; wishing I was wearing a substantial 1880s white bib apron and three petticoats, I bore it in from the kitchen on the yellow plate with the raised red flowers on the edge, the same plate we used at teatime in the sun room so long ago. A shimmering summer pudding is always greeted by Anglophiles with cries of delight, and so it was that afternoon.

Only three ingredients are needed to make such a pudding: fresh summer berries (in any combination), sugar, and good white bread. You line a deep bowl

We seldom get the very finest Darjeelings in the United States. The minute they are ready, they are privately jetted to Middle Eastern potentates. Other planes carry Darjeelings to be parachuted into Germany, where eager buyers wait below. Our very finest China teas are bought at the highest prices ($300 per pound and up) by certain men in Las Vegas. Caesar's Palace is a lavish customer. What does this mean?

Yunnan, *grown in what
is now thought to be the
very birthplace of tea, the
southern central part of
Yunnan province in China,
has such a mellow, all-
pervasive flavor that it has
been described by Norwood
Pratt, author of* The Tea
Lover's Treasury, *as
"God's own original." (He is
referring to the black tea,
not the earthy Pu-erh,
which has an almost truffle-
like appeal.) Perhaps this
divine black tea, my favorite,
is so delicious and satisfying
because, I believe, it is from
the original home of the
plant. Or perhaps, as Mr.
Pratt says, it is because it
has that peppery quality.*

with bread slices and pour in the berries, sugared and slightly cooked. As it chills overnight, the juices saturate the bread. When the bowl is inverted and removed, what emerges is an enormous, glossy, lovely, berry-colored jewel. Done perfectly, all the bread will be imbued with berry juice; but mine that day had a little bare spot. The English gentleman was sitting nearest the pudding, and he absentmindedly yet lovingly resauced it. We watched as he delicately and deliberately lifted the silver spoon and dribbled the sparkling berry juices over the bread. Then we listened as he described the summer blackberry puddings of his childhood in Sussex. He inclined his head to the side, still spooning sauce over the pudding, and a little quiet settled over the table; we were all with him in a quiet daydream of a perfect boyhood.

❧   ❧   ❧

Perhaps, in the end, the very smallest tea parties are the best. One afternoon, my wise old friend of twenty years, Camille—still recuperating after a long illness—stopped in to visit. It was impromptu, and there was no food to go with the tea, but that was the most "tea-ish" tea party I remember ever having, because it was the most elemental expression of the culture of tea: two kindred spirits together with their teacups and their mutual triumph over the trials of life.

It was late in the fall, one of those darkening afternoons that are the saddest times, according to the haiku poets. I brewed a pot of the exquisite Yunnan tea that Twinings had released that year, 1981, to celebrate their two hundred seventy-fifth anniversary. This was the quiet moment that I had been waiting for to share this new tea with a fellow tea lover and give it the attention it deserved. I hunkered down in my chair at the bare pine kitchen table. I was sad, too, that fall, and weak and dispirited; but I was cheered by seeing Camille again, sitting comfortably across the table, when not so long ago she had been so gravely ill.

Her deep brown eyes watched with mine as the fog seeped through the trees and swirled around the breakfast-nook bay window. As we sipped and savored our tea and talked, the recent events of our lives unfolded for us to consider. This Yunnan was good without milk, which anyway would have spoiled the beautiful color of the liquor. Its slight smokiness made it all the more warming and comfortable. After the second pot, we were finishing each other's sentences, and folding recent events right back up again, with all the problems aired out of them. Once again I had a perspective on where I was in life: in *a* place, not *the* place. Time never really stops, of course; I was in a place on my way through life, making my way to—somewhere.

I made another pot, and we admired the dry golden-tippy twisted leaves in the brilliant red tin. Then we admired the amber liquor in the cup. We both started to sweat. I made still another pot, and we grew giggly and a little dizzy, hanging on to chairs when we moved around a bit. Ah, this must be the famous "cup that cheers, but not inebriates!" I had heard of a "tea drunk": this must be it. But nothing was spinning; I felt safe and sequestered; my stomach was warm and well satisfied. Camille's eyes grew large when I suggested yet another pot. Did we dare? We did, and now I was floating, quite altered and refreshed. Camille seemed to have been fiercely strengthened. We were both happy.

After she left I tried to recall the eighth-century Chinese poem by the sage Lu Tong called "Thanks to Imperial Censor Meng for His Gift of Freshly Picked Tea." I got it out and read it again:

> One fable told about Yunnan is that long, long ago an advance man for the emperor was so deeply impressed by it that he requested a sample to send to the Son of Heaven. The peasants, who could not speak the Chinese of the imperial court, kept answering the advance man by making the gesture of cutting their own throats. After a time he understood: the emperor would like the tea and would want it all the time. But the tea was a first flush, and could only be supplied once a year. In his disappointed fury, the emperor would cut off the heads of the poor peasants. The tea was never sent, and some believe, as I do, that this accounts for the relative obscurity of this fabulous tea.

A good black Yunnan can have lots of twisted yellow gold leaves. Twinings Two Hundred Seventy-fifth Anniversary Tea did. But I have tasted superior Yunnans that were completely black.

The first bowl caresses my dry lips and throat,
The second shatters the walls of my lonely sadness,
The third searches the dry rivulets of my soul to find the stories of five
thousand scrolls.
With the fourth the pain of past injustice vanishes through my pores.
The fifth purifies my flesh and bone.
With the sixth I am in touch with the immortals.
The seventh gives pleasures I can hardly bear.
The fresh wind blows through my wings
As I make my way to Panglai.

The note below the poem explained that Panglai is understood not only to be the sacred mountain of that name, a place of Buddhist pilgrimage, but also to be a metaphor for Nirvana. I poured myself another cup and felt the wind in my wings.

RECIPES

My Trifle

The notion of a proper, stupendous trifle was planted in me by Stewart Brady, the San Francisco singing coaches' singing coach: "Darling, I build a trifle. It's the only way."

A trifle is best made three days before serving. It makes a terrific impression with very little effort—only one element needs to be cooked, the others can all be purchased—and you completely escape that nerve-racking, last-minute effort we should all strive to avoid.

For a first-class trifle, use as a base good-quality, plain panettone or buccellato *(no nuts or candied fruit); both are high-rising Italian yeast breads that are just next door to cake. Good-quality white bread, or a plain bakery white or yellow cake (dried out for a day or so, it will accept the sherry), can be substituted.*

The more eggs in the custard, the richer it will be. A commercial stove-top-cooked vanilla pudding can replace the homemade custard. Sometimes I prefer this, because it adds a delightful supersmoothness as a textural surprise.

Overdoing the jam, custard, cake, or nuts will do no harm, but being too generous with the sherry risks making a sloppy, alcoholic mess. Assemble the trifle in a large glass bowl if possible. Top with whipped cream as deep or shallow as you like. If strawberries are unavailable, garnish with another kind of berry.

First make the custard:

> 2 cups milk
> ½ cup sugar, or ⅓ cup honey
> 1 teaspoon vanilla
> Pinch of salt
> 2 to 4 eggs (go heavy on the yolks)

Preheat the oven to 325°F.

In a medium-size bowl blend together the milk, sugar or honey, and salt. Beat the eggs in another bowl and whisk them into the milk mixture. Lastly, add the vanilla.

Pour the custard into a small casserole or bread pan. Place in the oven in a larger pan and pour in enough hot water to come halfway up the sides of the pan holding the custard.

Bake for about 1 hour; when done, the center of the custard should tremble just a little when the pan is jiggled. Remove from the oven and set aside to cool while you start to assemble the trifle.

Next build the trifle:

Layer 1: In a large glass bowl, place finger-size pieces of panettone, *buccellato,* sponge cake, angel food cake, or good-quality white bread—enough to cover the bottom of the bowl. (You will need about 4 to 6 standard-size slices in all.) Sprinkle approximately 2 tablespoons of amontillado or any other nutty sherry over the slices.

Layer 2: Make another solid layer of the bread or cake pieces and spread all over with about ½ to ¾ cup red currant jelly or another assertively flavored jelly or jam.

Layer 3: Spoon about half the custard in dollops over the layer of jelly or jam and bread and evenly scatter 2 to 3 tablespoons of sliced almonds over all.

Layer 4: The mystical, telling layer—cut up about 2 cups fresh fruit in season. Nectarines and peaches are perfect, but almost any fruit, even bananas, will pinch-hit. (Not apples, though: they change the nature of the trifle too much.) Do not sugar the fruit.

Layers 5 through 7: Repeat layers 1 through 3, ending with the almonds. Cover and refrigerate for 2 to 3 days.

To serve: Whip a pint or so of heavy cream with about 1 tablespoon of sugar and 1 teaspoon vanilla (or less). When it forms soft peaks, spoon it over the top of the trifle and decorate with whole strawberries, washed and stemmed.

Dorothy Calimeris's Jam Cake

MAKES ONE 10-INCH-ROUND, 2-LAYER CAKE

Dorothy is famous for this cake. Almost anyone born in the thirties or forties will experience a wave of nostalgia when served a slice of it. Those born later can cultivate future nostalgia by baking it now. It's not hard to make, but be sure to use the tastiest jam you can find.

6 extra large eggs, room
    temperature
1 cup sugar
1 tablespoon vanilla, plus 2
    teaspoons for the cream
Grated zest of 1 lemon
½ cup unsalted butter, melted
    and cooled slightly

1 cup cake flour
½ cup confectioners' sugar
3 cups heavy cream
1 cup best-quality jam (I prefer
    raspberry)

Lightly butter a 10-inch springform cake pan and dust with flour. Preheat the oven to 350°F.

Separate the eggs. Put the whites in a large bowl and beat until soft peaks form. Gradually beat in ½ cup of the sugar and keep beating until the whites are thick and shiny. In another bowl, beat the egg yolks with the other ½ cup of sugar, the tablespoon of vanilla, and the lemon zest. Beat vigorously for 5 to 7 minutes (at high speed on an electric mixer), until the mixture is thick, light, and pale yellow. Gradually beat in the melted butter, pouring it into the bowl in a thin, steady stream. When the butter is completely incorporated, gently fold the yolk mixture into the egg white mixture.

Sift the cake flour over the mixture, ⅓ cup at a time, gently folding it in each time. Carefully pour or spoon the batter into the prepared pan and tap the pan on the counter several times to remove all the big air bubbles. Bake in the preheated oven for about 25 minutes. The cake should be a pale golden color. Do not overbake this cake or it will be rubbery. When it is done, remove from the oven and cool for 5 minutes in the pan. Gently run a knife around the edges of the pan, put the cake on a wire rack, remove the pan, and cool completely.

Add the confectioners' sugar and the 2 teaspoons of vanilla to the heavy cream and beat until soft peaks begin to form and the cream is spreadable. Split the cooled cake into 2 equal layers. Spread jam onto the bottom layer, keeping the jam within ½ inch of the cake's edge. Spread the cream frosting over the jam, making sure the the outer rim of the cake has a little extra frosting. (If the jam oozes through, it's okay—swirl it through the cream frosting for a pretty marbled effect. No one will know the difference!) Top with the other layer and cover the cake with the rest of the whipped cream frosting. Refrigerate until serving. The cake keeps fine in the refrigerator for 2 or 3 hours, but no longer or it may start to pick up refrigerator odors.

Lemon Helen's Lemon Tarts

MAKES EIGHT 3- TO 4-INCH TARTS

These tarts, my pride and joy, made a hit with the pastry cooks at Chez Panisse. And Alice called them "fantastic." If you can't get Meyer lemons (which you probably can't unless you live in California), use Eureka lemons (the common supermarket variety), but be sure to partially pare and slice them very *thin, and macerate the slices not just a few hours but overnight.*

LEMONS:

2 Meyer lemons
½ cup sugar
1 cup water

CRUST:

1 cup flour
1 tablespoon sugar
¼ teaspoon salt
¼ teaspoon grated lemon zest

½ cup butter, room temperature
1 tablespoon water
1 teaspoon vanilla extract

CUSTARD:

2 eggs
¼ cup sugar
1 teaspoon vanilla
1 cup milk

Hours ahead, or the night before, prepare the lemons. If they are Eureka lemons, grate about 2 teaspoons of lemon zest and reserve for the pastry and for sprinkling over the custard. Put the sugar and water in a saucepan, place over high heat, and cook, stirring constantly, until the sugar has dissolved. Bring the syrup to a boil and boil 2 minutes. Remove from the heat. Peel away all the rind and white pith from the lemons and slice them as thin as you can; it's okay if you have partial slices. Remove the pits. Place the lemon slices in the sugar syrup and macerate for at least 2 hours. If you can use Meyer lemons, simply remove seeds and slice very thin.

In a small bowl combine the flour, sugar, salt, and lemon zest. Add the butter and mix with your fingers or a pastry cutter until the mixture resembles coarse meal. Combine the water and vanilla extract and stir into the flour mixture, working just until the pastry forms a ball. Roll it up in plastic wrap and refrigerate 30 minutes.

While the dough is chilling, prepare the custard. Whisk together the eggs and sugar and beat until well blended. Whisk in the vanilla and milk, but do not overbeat or the custard will be too frothy.

Heat the oven to 350°F. Place the ball of dough on a floured board and roll it out about ¼-inch thick. Divide the dough into 8 pieces. Press them into 3- to 4-inch tart tins about 1 to 1½ inches deep. Trim off any overhang. Place tarts on a cookie sheet. Carefully pour the custard into the tart shells and gently pinch down the drained slices of macerated lemon into each tart. Sprinkle the reserved lemon zest over the tarts and bake until custard is only slightly jiggly, about 30 minutes.

Chapter Five

THE WATERS UPTON TEA ROOM

On an off-the-beaten-track San Francisco street, a street that was a dirty, dismal, nondescript, and lonely London gray, I found the tea room of my dreams. Far from the fashionable or even the friendly districts of the city, it was located in a Beaux Arts stucco hulk that had been built as a house of worship, but had until recently housed a School of Mortuary Science. Now, in its decay, it sheltered the Waters Upton Tea Room. It had the grim aspect of the scene of the crime in an Agatha Christie mystery. Dame Agatha would have played up its grotesquerie and given it a memorable name. The worn steps to the tea room on the side street entrance were grimy, strewn with leaves, and the door was ominously grilled. Even the sign needed paint.

A tinkling bell announced my entrance, instantly setting the mood of an English shop where all was quaint propriety and orderliness. Indeed, inside the tea room all was as clean and inviting as could be; there was not a whiff of shabbiness. The forbidding building outside was already forgotten, and so was the mess I had left behind at my home across the Bay. The room inhaled me into its warmth. No sign warned me Please Wait to Be Seated, so I promptly seated myself.

Several shy-looking middle-aged people were already seated. The room had a British separate-tables kind of formal informality. No one spoke. Rosy mahogany trim gleamed all around us; plain white curtains diffused the light, hiding any view of the dismal street outside; every table was graced with a glass vase, each one a different color and holding different kinds of flowers. I wondered who had the luxury of time for such details.

The unpretentiousness and comfort reminded me of an uncluttered sitting room of a particularly cheerful parsonage, where the parson's wife had fitted out everything to suit herself. The rug was exactly the same shade of baize green as the rug at Rutabaga's house in The Grove where we two girls had sprawled for hours fantasizing our lives as movie stars while memorizing great chunks of Gilbert and Sullivan just for fun. And this rug was even better, since it had a criss-crossing pattern of deep rose and white flowering vines. I could have stayed forever.

The hostess greeted me now in a marvelously maternal, firm Boston baritone. She then turned and handed an umbrella to an older man near me, saying, "I believe you left this yesterday." What a memory. What control—I was impressed. Suddenly I felt like an awkward, overgrown child whose possessions have to be looked after, but who is cared for ungrudgingly nevertheless. I was ready to cuddle up for my bedtime story. At the time I was over forty and had two children under the age of five. Anyone who has been in my shoes will recognize my readiness to regress. To get to my tea room, I had had to set out in driving rain, stop and get gas and money, cross the crowded Bay Bridge, snake through snarled traffic, search for a parking place—all the while ignoring my aching head and my cramping abdomen. I automatically suppressed the memory of my grandmotherly Norwegian baby-sitter's thin-lipped sneer at having had to come over to mind the children (the second day in a row—*and* at the last minute!), and banished all thoughts of the dying plants, the unwritten thank-you letters to the South Dakota relatives, the heaps of laundry left undone . . . I *had* to have a little order and quiet and comfort in my life. Before this afternoon, only in my dentist's waiting room had I felt the divine quiet that allowed my spirits to soar. (I was always hoping for the "Doctor is late today" refrain.) Now I was squirming with pleasure at snuggling into a chair where I could actually finish something—a cup of tea, a sentence, perhaps a sandwich. . . .

I picked up the menu, and now allowed myself to examine my hostess. Watching her patrol her tea room, I could see just how commanding a presence she was. She was small and straight and flat like a ballet mistress; her hair hung down round her thin face in a long, severe bob; her glasses hung round her neck down over her apron, which hung down over her tiny hips to her narrow skirt. She wore flat sensible shoes. Yet everything about her was up: she projected an inner joy from just being in that perfect room. She rarely smiled, but her every forceful movement radiated a sense of the joy in work. Her eyes shone as she surveyed her domain with the concentration of an orchestra conductor.

The sunny room was decorated with a wild variety of unmatched art—oils, watercolors, collages, macramé, mobiles—that had the look of a fond grandmother's collection, and my hostess moved through it all with a fond and possessive air: she owned the place. To me, who didn't know where the tuna fish was at home, she appeared to be the châteleine of a wondrous castle.

I returned to the menu, and read:

THE WATERS UPTON TEA ROOM STORY

Among the archives of a classical grand old dame, who was cared for in the last few years of her life by a friend of our Tea Room, was found an old magazine article entitled "The Tea Room I Did Not Have." It tells of a cheerful, creative young lady who plans every detail for a tea room but never opens it due to a sudden change in her life. The restoration of her plans and dreams was our inspiration as we developed our Waters Upton Tea Room. It is a pleasure to present to you these recipes restored from so long ago. We use the finest natural ingredients. All profits benefit the art/law educational programs of Student League of San Francisco, serving junior/senior high school students and their families since 1946.

Aha, I thought, that accounts for the art: the tea room must be a little showcase for the "art/law educational programs," although I did wonder where the law came in. And of course I wondered about the "cheerful, creative young lady." What was the mysterious change in her life? I imagined a sudden broken engagement (always a fascination for me) in Miss Havisham style. To find out just which of her plans and dreams were being restored, I read on through the list of specialties:

THE MOTORLOAF

A delicious, nutty whole-grained loaf filled with our delightful variety of individually wrapped finger sandwiches and garnished with our special spreads to enhance the consumption of the crust and make our Motorloaf your ultimate Epicurean delight.

LADY BALTIMORE CAKE

A famous old-fashioned favorite, richly flavored with marshmallow, almonds, and raisins, intimately filled and lusciously frosted to the satisfying of you, the finely tuned entrepreneurs of sweet treats.

DIPLOMATIC FRUIT PUNCH

A diplomacy of juices and fruits blended with sparkling soda for a gratifying refreshment.

Was I ready for enhanced crust consumption? Was I finely tuned enough for the satisfying of me? I yearned to qualify. But in my miserable state I dared not be too lavish. When the hostess appeared at my table, I ordered only Earl Grey tea, crumpets, and a modest baked apple.

In the blink of an eye, she returned with my teapot, a slightly chipped replica of a round green squash, with a dainty stemmed lid. Chips on teapots are

Earl Grey tea is probably the most popular afternoon tea in the Western hemisphere. Millions more pounds are sold of it than of any other tea. It is a solid choice for an afternoon tea because it has that light, piercing quality that is just assertive enough to set off sweets without intruding. A nutty, malty English Breakfast tea, to my way of thinking, is too heavy and too assertive with delicate sweets.

Twinings sells the most Earl Grey, followed by Halssen & Lyon of Germany, whose Earl Grey is wholesaled to many different dealers and carries no special designation. In third place is Drysdale's Earl Grey, which is very popular in England. There are at least twenty other Earl Greys, each of which has its devotees.

In 1983, a study done at the University of Wisconsin found that taking lemon with tea prevents it from interfering with the body's absorption of calcium and iron. Earl Grey is flavored with oil of bergamot, a citrus fruit native to Portugal. Could it be that the bergamot performs the same function as lemon, and that people prefer Earl Grey because they know unconsciously that it might be better for them?

endearing, or so I had been led to believe by Muttie, who always referred to her favorite teapot as "that sweet old thing." I looked at the nearby tables and saw quite a variety. There were lumpy Brown Bettys, an imitation black Wedgwood with a mismatched lid, a garish Aladdin's lamp, and a few pale pink heavy restaurant-ware teapots with lots of chips. It was somebody's second-best garage sale assemblage. Bravo, I thought, just my style—but not so fine a collection as to make me nervous or envious. I took off the lid of mine and looked in. Good news: loose leaves, still swirling about.

Besides the hostess herself, it was not quite clear who was waiting on the tables. From time to time a boy clad in an unironed white shirt and blue jeans with provocatively placed holes would emerge from the kitchen. Nearly oblivious to his surroundings, he would wade through the room, clearing a dish here or there and sometimes pouring a cup of tea. Probably an artist-in-the-making concentrating on his inner visions.

As I waited for my baked apple and continued my inspection of the room, I saw that it was actually composed of three adjacent rooms connected by sliding doors. Each room had its own gracefully vaulted ceiling. Through the open doors I could see through to the rear wall where an ivy-entwined white trellis provided a visual climax to the carpet. This style of green-and-white decor, in vogue again today, had been popular in the forties, but in the seventies it was wildly out of fashion. In front of the trellis was a white table stacked with a rainbow of different-colored tea tins. The whole effect was inviting, but it began to dawn on me that these rooms had probably been the old viewing rooms for the dear departed, and the little kitchen off behind the trellis would have been the preparation room.

The hostess wheeled round the corner from the kitchen as if she were on a rolling platform and set my baked apple down before me housed in a sturdy soup bowl; it was still warm and surrounded by a pool of thick cream. The baked apple is the elephant rag doll of desserts: ugly and wrinkled, but sweet and well-loved. How fine for this tea room to offer a dessert most restaurants shun because of its disheveled appearance. I have always maintained that it takes a calm and centered psyche to appreciate a plain baked apple. A baked apple can be elevated to giddy heights by adding walnuts, cinnamon, honey, and pieces of sugared orange rind; but a plain warm baked apple deep in cream can be just as enchanting, seducing one into a quiet sensual world with the first bite through its skin into the homely sweetness of its chiffonlike interior. I calmed myself and gave the tea room two more marks, then tried to catch the eye of my new heroine and demonstrate somehow that she had an appreciative customer, but she was gone. In the secret-garden part of my mind, I began to call my hostess "herself" in the old Irish way.

I had just finished my apple when she returned with an evangelical look in her eye, a stack of napkins in one hand topped with one of those compact little plastic pillows of blue ice, and, balanced in the other, a knife and a very large loaf of nut bread. She stationed herself at a small rolling table behind me that was draped with so much white linen that it suggested a cross between a child's doll bed and an operating table for a surgical procedure in a well-kept Catholic hospital. First she peeled back napkins from the mattresslike mound on the table, placed the ice pack on top, and replaced the linen. A pause for consideration, and then she added a few more napkins. She then tenderly positioned the loaf on top, and stepped back to admire and calculate. A pause, then she carefully began to make cuts into the loaf. It looked as if she was carving out a shape of some kind—a boat, a ship, a bathtub? I kept craning around to watch this perfor-

The oldest-known flavored tea is jasmine. Its flowers were added to tea as early as A.D. 1100, possibly to cover up moldy flavors that might develop in shipment and to stretch the tea. (Bergamot-flavored tea is almost unknown in China.)

Charles, Earl Grey, was an English diplomat who is supposed to have received this recipe from a mandarin in gratitude for saving his son's life. Whatever the truth of this tale, in 1830, a bergamot-flavored tea blend of this name was introduced by Jackson's of Piccadilly, a shop around the corner from the earl's house in London.

mance, and finally asked, "What is it you are making?" Silence; she was intent on her job. Then, louder, I blurted out, "I'll have some!" She spun around.

"Yes? Some Motorloaf?" she said, her eyes opening wide as she enunciated the word. She leaned forward and the explanation poured out; the deep voice was raised slightly: "You see, it is a motorcar—the inside is carved out and cut into slices. Sandwiches are made, and then replaced inside the cavity, where they become seats, as you can see." She demonstrated. "Further cuttings are made to represent wheels." Here she cut out circles. "And these are positioned at the four corners of the motorcar." She did so, looking up at the ceiling as if remembering her lines, or perhaps reliving a cherished memory. "Formerly, when one motored, as driving was called long ago, one occasionally longed for a bite or two, and the motorloaf was made to fit neatly over the central drive shaft, between the seats. So convenient for one." She picked up the loaf carefully and showed me the finished nut-bread touring car. "And *this,* of course, keeps it all cool!" she said triumphantly, peeling back the napkins and exposing the blue ice pack. Of course.

"And now, some Motorloaf? A chicken sandwich, perhaps? Or a plain bread-and-butter?" For the first time she smiled and looked at me invitingly.

"Yes, oh yes—the chicken, please," I replied almost tongue-tied.

My little sandwich was moist, dark, delicious, and utterly satisfying, thanks to the excellence of the nut bread, the absence of extraneous elements, the high proportion of dark meat to light, and a light touch with the mayonnaise. I

had one hand on the sandwich and the other on my cup of Earl Grey, and emulated my farmer uncles: a bite, a slurp, a bite, a slurp—a technique that enhances whatever is being consumed, but which can be tricky in public. Children eat and drink like this; they know best. The Earl Grey was a bit stronger now, and tea and sandwich were in perfect balance. The old reliable Earl Grey, I reflected, really *can* be the best with tea treats; it's light and yet just piercing enough to make a comfortable, slightly acidic statement. And it's a tea that never intrudes. Inhaling cup after cup, I vaguely realized it was an excellent Earl Grey, but was too immersed in the pleasures of the combination of tea and food to ask, or care, what it was. And never once did I let up on the eating and slurping rhythm; my uncles would have been proud of me. That Earl Grey, that day, just got to work and did its job—to lift me up and settle me down at the same time.

As I pondered my choices on the compact menu, I wondered what the history was of this woman who could preside over such a pleasant, smooth-running room, make such perfect nut bread, and handle so much napery? I flagged the holey young man and ordered the trifle.

After a moment he returned and slid the plate in front of me, as if releasing a bowling ball onto the table. The trifle had been spooned onto the plate. My serving was about the size of a baseball; it was unsullied by any sauce and topped with a lone maraschino cherry. Before he could make his getaway, I saw I needed a spoon, and asked for one. He froze, then rubbed his hands together nervously, and looked to the ceiling for assistance. It was a dark moment for him. He lurched behind the trellis, and there was a long pause. My eye caught a line on the menu I had overlooked: "The Tea Room is staffed by volunteers dedicated to supporting the programs of our Student League." I had a strong suspicion that my young man's dedication had been volunteered by his principal. I took the delay to look about me, and noticed several customers. One, the woman at the next table, had a black-and-white stuffed animal with her with which she appeared to be having a conversation. Another, a man, crouched over his food with a hunted expression. A haven for all of us, I thought.

Suddenly we heard a small crash of cutlery. Then the volunteer emerged with an innocent smile on his face and proudly produced what I'd asked for. It was a fork actually, but I went right to work with it.

One bite and I started to look for my hostess. I had eaten almost half my trifle, one eye cocked for her, before she tooled by. "This is really a proper English trifle," I gushed. She nodded, about to move on. "This is the best I've ever had in America! When did you make it?"

"Friday," she answered. And this was Tuesday. No wonder it was so good: it had been laced with nutty sherry and properly aged. I wanted to talk more with her, this giver of sanity and calm and relaxation, but she had her eye on the latticework and slipped behind it.

I was quite full, but out of a nervous high, and all pains forgotten, I began ordering more tea. That young man definitely knew how to pour. I drank down several cups in a row, pondering my next move, and began to break out in what tea cognoscenti know as a "tea sweat." The room became very bright and close. I was stuffed but couldn't imagine ever wanting to leave. Finishing off the last of my second or third pot of tea, I saw over the edge of my cup a piece of cake being delivered to the next table. Lusciously frosted, and presumably "intimately filled," it could only be the famous Lady Baltimore Cake. The hostess material-ized at tableside. More tea? Anything else? I took a deep breath, and threw cau-tion to the wind: "Yes, Lady Baltimore Cake, please." I had a devil-may-care vision of myself—tearing through forests, leaping, sweating, racing to the edge of a cliff; swallowing caution, pounding it down into my black inner passion and throwing myself in a paroxysm of anguished delight into a tea-dark sea. Noth-ing mattered but that cake.

I cannot describe it with sufficient precision. Its icing was the texture of powdered snow; layers of cake much like the wedding cakes of my childhood, al-ways wrapped in a paper napkin to take home, to make a wish and dream on. And the filling with nuts and figs was irresistible. It brought to mind an elegant Southern parlor with white ruffled curtains and mahogany furniture. It made me feel like a lady, and was a fitting climax. (It was the "piece of resistance," to use the favorite phrase of a pal of Mother's, a lady who always delivered it with a heavy Oklahoma twang. The other famous line of Mrs. Oklahoma was her reply when asked what kind of china she wanted from France: "I don't care, as long as it's Lim-oh-jeez.")

After the cake I was exhausted and the bladder called. (In our house it was always "the," not "my," bladder.) Feeling a little dizzy from all the excitement, I got to my feet unsteadily and asked the hostess the way to the W.C. (showing off how English I was), but she didn't seem to notice.

"Just follow 'round the way, through the door. You'll see the sign." I've learned the hard way that "'round the way" is a sloppy Briticism; I headed through the doorway and down the dark hallway, gripping the wall. It was like a slightly scary trip to the cool, mysterious basement of a new friend's house in my childhood days. After fumbling around a bit I found the facilities, and shortly thereafter made my way back, feeling more than a little threatened by my excursion. It was wonderful to find my old buddies back there in the bright, warm tea room, my separate tablemates, eating and sipping away, alive and well.

I sighed and settled down. Was it time to leave? I didn't want to think about it. The woman at the next table, who was sportily dressed and sturdily built, rose and went 'round the way to the back as I had done. When she returned, she approached and invited me to her table to meet her little stuffed animal. I did, nodding appreciatively to her tiny companion, all still and glassy-eyed. I suddenly recalled that the tea room was not far from a major psychiatric hospital. The place went up one more mark in my estimation. I was introduced, quite properly and pleasantly: "This is Monium, my panda. He's very good company." It seemed like a good moment to leave.

I must have paid the bill and left; all I remember is crossing the bridge in a kind of trance. Afterward I was to escape to the Waters Upton on many an afternoon. It never lost its atmosphere of off-center Anglophilia. The amateur artworks on the walls changed periodically; the volunteers came and went; but my hostess remained steadfast and true, never wavering in the pursuit of her marvelous idiosyncratic vision.

The tea room closed without warning in 1986, just days after a handsome review appeared in the Sunday magazine section of the paper. On the padlocked door was a sign: Closed/Re-opening Soon. It never did. The thunderbolt closing was fittingly absurd, at first, and then a comfort. At least it would never change for the worse, and I still have my overheated memories. My friends and I can reminisce like alumni and pretend that we have never given up hope that one day the Waters Upton Tea Room will rise again, phoenixlike, salubrious and sublime.

RECIPES

These recipes re-create the taste and spirit of the delights I found at the Waters Upton Tea Room; the originals remain, in Bostonian fashion, a family secret.

Motorloaf Nut Bread

MAKES 1 LOAF

1½ cups graham flour (or
   whole wheat flour)
¾ cup all-purpose flour
2 teaspoons baking powder
½ teaspoon salt
¼ teaspoon baking soda

1½ cups sour milk (or yogurt or
   buttermilk)
⅓ cup dark molasses
3 tablespoons butter, melted
½ cup chopped walnuts

Preheat the oven to 350°F. Grease a 4×8-inch or a 5×9-inch bread pan.

Mix together all the dry ingredients in a large bowl, lifting and tossing with a fork. Stir in the milk, molasses, and melted butter. Mix thoroughly, but do not beat. Incorporate the walnuts and transfer the dough to the greased pan. Bake in the preheated oven for about 45 minutes.

The Noble Baked Apple

First, buy the heaviest, tastiest cream available. Then select a hard, tasty apple (Granny Smith, Rome Beauty, Yellow Delicious, Gravenstein, or any other with a firm texture).

Preheat the oven to 375°F.

Core the apple. In its center, put about ¼ teaspoon of butter, a pinch of cinnamon, and a little brown sugar, to taste.

Place the apple in a baking pan and bake for 30 minutes or more. When the apple's skin splits, and it looks lumpy and in need of a hug, it is ready. Serve warm, or at room temperature, with a generous amount of cream poured around it.

Lady Baltimore Cake

MAKES ONE 8-INCH 3-LAYER CAKE

CAKE:

1 cup sugar

¾ cup butter, room temperature

1¾ cups cake flour

2 teaspoons baking powder

½ cup milk

½ teaspoon almond extract

3 egg whites

¼ teaspoon salt

FROSTING:

2 cups heavy cream

¼ cup powdered sugar

1 teaspoon vanilla

6 dried figs, chopped

½ cup plump raisins, chopped

1 cup chopped pecans, or 1 cup
    slivered almonds

Preheat the oven to 350°F. Grease three 8-inch round cake pans with a little butter and dust with flour.

Beat the sugar and the butter together until light and fluffy. In a separate bowl, sift together the cake flour and baking powder. Combine the milk and the almond extract. Add the milk alternately with the flour and baking powder to the butter and sugar mixture; the batter will be thick.

In a clean bowl, beat the egg whites with the salt until they form soft peaks. Fold the egg whites into the batter. Divide the batter among the prepared cake pans. Bake in the preheated oven for 25 to 35 minutes, or until a toothpick inserted in the middle comes out clean. Remove from the oven, cool for 5 minutes, and then invert onto racks and allow to cool completely before frosting.

To make the frosting, whip the cream with the powdered sugar and vanilla in a large mixing bowl until stiff enough to spread. Reserve ⅓ of the whipped cream in a smaller bowl. Fold the figs, raisins, and nuts into the whipped cream remaining in the larger bowl. Assemble the cake, spreading half the cream mixture between the first and second layers, and the other half between the second and third. Use the reserved plain whipped cream to frost the top. Chill until ready to serve.

Chapter Six

My Early Days at Chez Panisse: Converting the Heathen

I fell into the food world when little islands of time began to open up in my life as a new/old mother. I'd become a regular at The Swallow, a collective newly opened in the art museum at the University of California. This upscale cafeteria had spun off from The Cheese Board, a collective which was now across the street from Chez Panisse and selling, as one wag put it, "one thousand unnecessary cheeses." One day at lunch I heard my friend Camille, one of The Swallow founders, say, "Oops, no one to front the counter tomorrow." She turned to me with a wild surmise. The next day I made myself useful by taking over the counter—running the cash register, serving food, chatting with everyone, and being a sort of hostess. I loved it, and stayed almost ten years.

Alice Waters often came in to eat. Her friend Tom Luddy, now a film producer, then the director of the Pacific Film Archive, had hired me to plan and host a film party. So when Alice asked him if he knew anyone who could step in as weekend host in the new café upstairs at Chez Panisse, he suggested me as the pinch hitter. It was the same story: a *click*, as something fell into place.

My tea life at Chez Panisse began innocuously enough in the spring of 1980.

Alice and I were standing by the bar, chatting. I said, "Our Earl Grey tea is good, but it's made with lavender. The traditional flavoring is oil of bergamot."

"*Do* something about it then," she said, clamping my forearm with her tiny hand. This urgent admonition would start my tea "career" as similar incidents did for scores of cooks, bakers, farmers, and fishmongers over the years.

The moment at the bar flowed quietly by without my taking much notice, but soon after this short exchange I drifted around the corner to our pace-setting neighborhood coffee and tea place, run by the handsome, charismatic, Dutch-born Alfred Peet. The shop had opened in 1966, five years before Chez Panisse, and we took as scripture whatever Mr. Peet (a decade or so our senior) said about that strong coffee and tea of his. I bought some Assam, I think, and returned to the restaurant, where I found a Mason jar *and* a lid for it (no small achievement in the early chaotic days of the café kitchen) and told a few bussers to keep an eye on our new tea. I didn't change the Earl Grey after all—it was from Peet's—but my tea-buying days had begun.

The taste of the tea we were producing at the café kept nagging at me, though. It wasn't quite right. I had a cup or two every day before I plunged into my long seven-hour stretch of greeting and seating. The café, above the more formal dining room, had been a success from the day it opened. The bar area was often as jammed as a five o'clock subway car in Manhattan, and some customers would wait hours for a table. We seemed to be at the vortex of the universe. I became known for stuffing my tips into my bra: ten-dollar bills on the left, and twenties on the right. We had lots of attention, and the money flowed. It was a wild and heady time. Way past the midnight closing hour, after a busy night, the gang "on the floor" (as we described our workspace; we should have said "on stage") would gather round the bar, winding down from it all by consuming several bottles of Champagne. No one got to sleep before four or five in the morning. When things eventually began to calm down I began to fuss about the tea. While lavish attention was devoted to every whorl of foam topping the cappuccinos, tea was being slapdashed.

I knew that tea leaves had to be immersed and fully infused, swirling around in freshly boiling water brought from cold to the boiling point—that

The enemies of tea are, in order of their threat: damp, heat, light, and air. Good tea should be stored like a fine spice: in a tightly closed container, away from heat and light. Ceramic canisters with spring-type sealing lids are best. Metal containers with tightly fitting lids are next best.

then and only then would the essence locked up in the fermented, twisted leaves be released. The leaves do indeed look as if they are in agony; they also look a bit as if they are searching for that release.

But there I was—stuck. How could the agony take place? The espresso machine dispensed none-too-fresh water at about 190°F, too far from the boiling point. I called the company that took care of the machine and met a serviceman early one Saturday morning, before anyone else had come in. I told him to crank up the temperature as close to boiling as he could. In a moment, genial as could be, he told me, "I got her up there about as far as she'll go. You be careful now she don't get too high or she'll explode." I backed down, and he just as genially reset the control.

Next I tried sabotage. I came in early again, disconnected the spigot from the machine, and hid it. By the next day there was pandemonium. The cooks were indignant: they needed that water to make themselves a quick cup of tea in the morning! I pointed out the twelve stove burners on which they could boil water and refused to search for the spigot. But a few weeks later, it was replaced. I pretended not to notice.

Spiffy as the espresso machine was for coffee, for tea it was no better than the old glass urns in the usual restaurant. Then I remembered the electric tea kettle some people used in their homes. It has a little button that pops out when the water comes to a boil. Why not use some of them at the café? Keats's Cortés couldn't have been happier with his discovery than I was with mine. I bought two, one each for the front and back bus stations. But Chez Panisse occupies an old house with wiring that has been added to, patched, and rerigged countless times. It took over three months of cajoling to get proper three-pronged outlets for my new little kettle darlings. Once they were plugged in, I had to face the problem of fresh water. I decided it would be pushing my luck to demand plumbing in the front bus station, and settled for replenishing the kettle from the frequently refilled water pitchers, refilling them "as often as possible."

> The water from an espresso machine is only a little better than the water from the usual coffee shop setup with the three familiar clear glass urns: black handle for regular coffee, orange handle for decaf, and another black handle for the unmistakable globe of plain water behind the smudgy glass. That water is for what passes as tea: a warm, weak beverage taken out of a bag. And that water sits for hours, getting staler and flatter, losing more and more oxygen. As the oxygen evaporates, so does the chance of having tea, as it is the oxygen in the water that breathes the life and flavor into the leaves.

But the kettles had problems. The short cords, fine for home use, become maddening if you are in a bus station with a dozen things to do that very minute. The button pops out to tell you the water is ready to pour, but if you are clearing a table, even if it is only ten feet away, you might as well be in Philadelphia.

I expected the bussers to watch carefully for the moment of the boil, the pop of the button; and, of course, they should refill the kettles every time. I was dreaming. In Europe I had seen machines that produce freshly boiled water at the touch of a finger, but they are too large and expensive for our café. Every time the handle is depressed, fresh water is pulled from the wall pipe, which is frequently, but at Chez Panisse, tea orders don't come in that often. Harrod's in London has such a machine. It's called a closed still, it's over a hundred years old, and it works perfectly. I watched the waiters there put loose dry tea in their pots, load up their trays, and zip past the still, stopping just long enough to fill the teapot with that bubbly, glistening stream of steaming, freshly boiled H_2O! I was jealous. Why all this fuss for these few essentials?

Alas, we have become accustomed to stale water with a tea bag whisked through it. The English writer Dermot Purgarie put it superbly when he said that when you order tea in America, "they bring you a noxious brown bag floating in lukewarm iodine."

As you pour from a kettle, look for that thick stream of water, bubbly looking and glistening, fresh and vigorous—water with plenty of oxygen in it to start the agony.

> *A friend of mine who grew up alongside a samovar has only one way to describe water proper for tea: "A mad boil." In the same forceful way she never says rolls or toast must be hot, or very hot. They must be "hot-hot-hot!" This is pronounced as much as possible like a one-syllable sound of intense excitement, about no matter how dull a bun. . . .*
>
> *The quaint old fiction of the kettle simmering all day on the hearth, waiting to be turned into a delicious cup of tea, is actively disturbing to anyone who cares very much whether his tea will be made from lively water instead of a liquid . . . which is flat, exhausted, tasteless—in other words, with the hell cooked out of it. . . .*
>
> *It is safe to say that when the water boils, as it surely will, given enough heat under it, it is ready. Then, at that moment and no other, pour it into the teapot. . . . If it cannot be used then, turn off the heat and start over again when you yourself are ready; it will harm you less to wait than it will the water to boil too long.*
>
> —M. F. K. Fisher

Good tea requires only a few things:

1. Good-quality dry loose tea, long-leafed and tightly rolled or twisted, or short-leafed and expertly produced.
2. Good-quality, freshly drawn cold water.
3. Pots that are cleaned and rinsed without the use of heavy soaps or detergents.
4. Loving care from the moment of purchase until the tea is poured from the tin or canister. Damp is tea's worst enemy, followed by heat, light, and air. (Clear glass containers won't do because they allow light in.)
5. Milk (not half-and-half and not cream, which is reserved for Ost-friesen tea), lemon, and sugar (raw, brown, or refined).

These are the basic requirements for making black tea—easy to meet at home, not so easy to achieve in a restaurant.

Chez Panisse may give the impression of being a charming little restaurant, but we serve over four hundred people a day upstairs in the café and another hundred in the fancier dining room downstairs at dinnertime. There are over a hundred people on the staff. Making sure that all was being done properly when I was only there two or three days a week was very much like teaching people how to brush their teeth by long-distance telephone.

One day I found a two-pound bag of tea, top wide open, lean-ing against the wall of the brick pizza oven (getting hotter and staler every moment). My stomach went tight. I am less than graceful about this. Lady Jane (a label my mother stuck on me when I was being imperious) *will* have her way. The cords on my neck stand out, and as one veteran busser says, "I know that wound-up look; I can spot it at fifty yards." Once a new busser told me proudly that he had filled the kettle with warm water from the tap. "It takes less time that way!" he said, beaming. I was

> In general, teapots should be washed with clear water, or with an occasional drop of detergent. Never use harsh cleansers or clogging, clinging soap. Use a little baking soda in the wash water every so often if you feel the pot is too black. Unless the blackish deposit is extremely heavy, it will not affect the tea. In Yixing teapots used for oolong a residue is considered desirable.

apoplectic. "You have to start with cold water and bring it to the boil, otherwise nothing happens!" I marched off stage right, afraid of my own violence. That day it wasn't the tea that was in agony.

I kept trying. A meeting might work, a formal meeting. In midafternoon, the downstairs dining room is filled with little meetings. In one corner the forager and the café cooks are tasting olive oils, on the porch a pastry chef is being interviewed, and in another corner the downstairs kitchen crew in their still-fresh whites are fine-tuning the night's menu. I decided to call a meeting, too, and announced a bussers' meeting at 3:30 P.M., just half an hour before staff meal. One young man showed up, late, waited with me for a few minutes, then drifted off to his dinner. And, after a few more minutes, my time was up.

I posted memos and announcements and notices, and began the nibbling approach. I offered cups of tea to staff and asked them to taste. I talked tea and told tea anecdotes whenever I could, while hanging out before and after work. I raved about the tea I was having at home, hoping to make them jealous. I gave them tea to take home. I was zealous. Often I would go in on Sunday when the restaurant was closed and only the garde-manger taking inventory would be there. If the teapots had not been cleaned and stacked correctly, I'd call the dishwashers at home to remind them how to do it. I leave to the reader's imagination the effect of such a phone call the morning after a ten-hour shift in the heat and tension of the dishroom on a Saturday night.

After I had a tea list I was proud of, the quiet push was on. I asked the charming Alfred Peet to lunch at the café. It was time for a little outside praise. His knowledge of tea was eye-opening. Asked to identify two Darjeelings, he correctly ascertained that they were the same tea, but one was a year older than the other. He smelled, tasted, and slurped. (I learned how a tea taster brings the tea across the top of the tongue in a rapid whoosh that caused heads at nearby tables to turn.) He patted the leaves onto his face, just to be certain. He left saying I had a small but distinguished list. "And be patient," he added. "It will take ten years to elevate the taste." He'd made an effect. And he was right; it did take ten years.

I kept chipping away at the problem with the water. When things were a

Milk must be used for ordinary black teas; half-and-half will overwhelm the morning cuppa. Synthetic nondairy cream and milk substitutes should be banished forever.

little slow one afternoon, I noted that the kettle had been slumbering away, unfilled for over an hour; I made our house peach tea with the old stale water and offered a taste of it to small group of bussers, as a "new" tea. "Hmmm, well, this is okay, but it tastes a little medicinal. . . . What is it?" Then I made it again with fresh boiling water. "*Wow!* What *is* this, it's terrific! It's delicious!" My point was made. But still the bussers would not put fresh water in the kettle often enough. Too much trouble!

I remember waking one morning from a bad dream and clapping my hand to my forehead. A little squiggly cartoon figure in my brain kept screaming, "HOW CAN IT BE SO HARD TO BOIL WATER IN ONE OF THE NATION'S MOST PRESTIGIOUS RESTAURANTS?!"

About a week later, part of the answer came from one of the bussers, a quiet young man with a Gibson girl's best-beau kind of handsomeness: a perfectly shaped F.D.R. head covered with close-set blond curls. His name was John Norton. He sauntered over to me one day and said, as if resuming an interrupted conversation, "Now Helen, I think we can work out this tea kettle thing." I was all ears. "The bussers get busy and use stale water, right?"

"Right, they won't take the time to refill," I wailed.

"They probably never will," he replied, and paused for dramatic effect. I

forgave him. "But, if we ask them to do something only *half* way, something quick, they just might do it."

"They might." (I doubted it.)

"So, if we ask them to add just a short shot of water before putting on the kettle, at least some of the water will be fresh. It won't be perfect, but it'll be better."

"Of course! That's what we'll do!" And that's what we still do. When an order for tea comes in and it's a crazy lunchtime, the busser simply adds a little cold water, waits a few seconds, and when the water comes to the boil and the button pops out, he pours. A sensible and humane compromise. As far as I know, no other restaurant takes that much trouble with their tea service.

With the annual Chez Panisse staff retreat coming up, John and I decided to pitch our new methodology at the grand get-together. The staff retreat that year was a major event, a day of talk and inspiration and warm group feeling at a beautiful winery in the Napa Valley. Alice grilled her fabulous hamburgers, and her husband, Stephen, set them off with his double-fried french fries. The pastry department had made ice cream *and* ice cream cones. After lunch, John and I planned to make our pitch. We had even come up with a little song, complete with guitar accompaniment, to the tune of "Java Jive":

> *I love coffee, I love tea,*
> *I love the kettle time and it loves me,* {here we swung the kettles}
> *Norton's gonna show ya,*
> *Just how you can pour ya,*
> *A cuppa, cuppa, cuppa, cuppa tea!*

We even had straw hats.

Though only a small portion of those hungry folks focused on us and not lunch, the little ditty seems to have helped. A zap of cold water makes all the difference in how the tea tastes—and how Lady Jane sleeps at night.

Chapter Seven

LATTER DAYS
AT CHEZ PANISSE:
PREACHING TO THE CHOIR

Gradually—very gradually—the tide of battle turned as those opposed to tea or simply careless with it began to see that, yes, a first-class restaurant ought to serve the best teas and serve them well.

By this time Lady Jane had become Lady Teasdale for my implacable determination to preserve the integrity of each tea we served. I regularly offered training sessions for new bussers—or whoever was inclined to see what the bees in Lady T's bonnet were all about. One issue of *Chez News,* our in-house newsletter, featured a cartoon of a space-suited me gesturing wildly to a small group of puzzled space aliens, their little antennae quivering. The caption, "Helen Giving Tea Seminars on the Moon," was a dig, but a cute one. I smiled and pressed on.

One of my best successes was iced peach tea using a peach tea I discovered at Freed, Teller & Freed, an old—even venerable—shop selling tea and coffee. This peach had been created in Germany by rotating black tea in a large oak barrel with a tiny amount of essence drawn from real fruit, not synthesized chemically. Several hours of this blending produces a tea that truly brings on the taste of summer.

Darjeelings are expensive, but they have a certain sparkle and they are so flexible they will accompany any food or sweet. Perhaps this is why they are so often compared to Champagne. If in doubt, buy the most expensive (garden, not brand). Tea is one of the last strongholds in the marketplace where expense and quality still go together.

This emphatically flavored iced tea was an instant hit with both staff and customers. Servers were quick to carry out the instructions I posted: "If a customer asks for a slice of lemon, say, 'I will bring it if you insist, but please try the tea first. The lemon will kill this tea.'"

Among the bussers, "getting the peach right" became a serious game. One morning I stopped in front of a gaggle of them chatting at the pizza oven before plunging into their set tasks. The peach had been made. I took a taste, looking over these refugees from an Our Gang comedy. "Which of you is responsible for this iced tea?" Pushing and shoving; then the newest busser stepped forward.

"I did it," he said nervously.

"It's perfect," said I with a rush of good feeling. The gang roared with laughter and clapped the newcomer on the back.

By now I was ordering more and more teas. Tim Castle of Intra-Trade Company in Los Angeles came up to visit his old haunts and dropped off some samples. He was casually elegant, and so were his teas. I started to learn what really expensive, superior teas can taste like, especially the Darjeelings from the foothills of the Himalayas in India, the Champagne of teas. I learned the word for the growth seasons: the "flushes." I liked to imagine the tea leaves being magically flushed out of the gardens, and loved the connotation of blushing and leafing out. I tried an autumnal third-flush Darjeeling for the first time, one so evocative of the season that I can recall exactly where I was standing in my kitchen looking at the Bay bridge on the October day that I took my first sip.

Good-quality peach tea from a northern German auction is the only fruit-flavored tea I'm crazy about. Pay the highest price possible in a good tea shop, and you'll be assured of good quality. The peach flavor is often compared to the muscat flavors of Darjeeling teas. It is very good hot, but overbrewed it becomes medicinal. Save it for iced tea, and never add anything to it. (Many Darjeelings are said to have a peachy aftertaste, and peach is much more compatible with tea than raspberry or some other contrasting astringent fruity flavor.)

That Darjeeling was so good that I asked some of the new Chez employees to stop by for a tasting. Peter Steiner, the new waiter, came, and so did a few others. I hadn't planned ahead and had no tea treat, but I had bread and butter, so I could serve pepper toast. Just one tea—the perfect autumnal Darjeeling—and one thing to eat—buttered toast peppered right from a café pepper shaker. We were six, crowded around our table in the bay window of my kitchen. The weather was brilliant and clear, and our spirits were high. I got out my biggest teapot. As I was pouring the handle broke—but I caught it before *all* the tea was spilled. We laughed, cleaned up the mess, and tried my second-biggest teapot. Its straw handle slipped out of place. More spillage. We coped and laughed and ate many toasts. I asked Peter to help me make a fresh pot but he poured the water too soon, before it had boiled—he was a coffee drinker—and we teased him without mercy. I took a deep breath and made a final pot with care. As we downed it in quiet concentration, the delicate strength of the tea began to pull us together. By ones and twos we got up and went out for walks around the neighborhood, the lovely post-Darjeeling furriness still tickling our tongues and caressing the roofs of our mouths. Toast and tea—such good companions. And that fall day they had led to the informal, and the warmth, of my kind of tea time.

In 1988, a good year for Darjeelings, I bought a rare one from Tom Kaplan of Caffe Latte in Los Angeles. I tasted it in his café, loved it, and bought lots of it: four hundred dollars' worth. I offered it for tea in the dining room downstairs and thought it would last for months. Paul Bertolli, our head chef, was crazy about it; he said it made him feel like the top of his head was coming off. "Wonderful, wonderful!" he kept murmuring. When he returned from a two-week vacation, he made himself a pot using the same amount he was used to. But this time the brew was so intense and nearly bitter that he was almost sickened. That was when I learned how fast a truly fine tea can mature and change. I regretted the wasted money, but I managed to sell some of it to a neighboring restaurant, advising them that it could be cut with some innocuous blander tea—a neutral inexpensive Nilgiri, for example.

The labyrinthine study of Darjeelings can be all-absorbing. Comparisons of gardens and good and bad years can lead to a heady blend of connoisseurship,

The word flush *applies to the first budding growth of the tea leaf. The first flush comes in late April, the second in midsummer, and the third in the fall. Many tea folks prefer the autumnal teas, because they are as astringent and puckery as the others yet seem to have a mellower flavor.*

If you buy a very expensive Darjeeling, drink it up within a month or so; keeping qualities vary and character can sometimes change quickly.

Ostfriesen teas may be
made up of as many
as eighteen to twenty-five
different teas, most of them
Assams. The blender uses as
many as necessary to duplicate the exact flavor of the
formula.

If Darjeelings are the
Rolls-Royces of the tea
world, Ceylons are the
robust, familiar, dependable
Chevrolets. Grown in Sri
Lanka (which used to be
called Ceylon, and before
that, the Isle of Serendip) at
three thousand to four
thousand feet above sea level,
they produce the short-
leafed, bright, brisk
Lipton-type teas we all
know and love.

Chests of tea still exist as a unit of measurement. Some are wooden boxes banded with tin and others are round cardboard containers. Good-quality tea is sold by the half-chest. The peach tea we order for Chez Panisse from tea broker Mike Spillane arrives special delivery—always causing a little stir.

A half-chest quality tea weighs from 50 to 90 pounds; supermarket-quality "bag" teas are sold by the chest and weigh from 80 to 130 pounds.

---

pleasure, and one-upmanship. The names alone are enchanting. Many gardens are named for their owners' dreams of success. Did Margaret of the famous Margaret's Hope garden ever know how celebrated her husband's garden would become? Did the garden called My Own stay that way? Did Mr. Dan of Dan's Land exult in ownership?

The most consistently famous garden is Castleton, a proud English name. One day in Berkeley, Jim Reynolds, the manager of Peet's, mentioned to me that he had a chest of Castleton in the back of the store. He didn't plan to sell it outright (far too expensive!), but to use it to perk up blends of his own. We looked at each other for a moment, and then in the same millisecond our feet hit the floor and we raced to the back just to look at it. A tea chest like that has a turn-of-the-century look: the heavy wooden box, about three and a half feet wide and three feet deep, is banded with tin and boldly stenciled in black, C.A.S.T.L.E.T.O.N.

It never occurred to me to order from just one tea company because there were so many interesting people in the food world coming through the door, worldwide travelers who could be persuaded to add to our list. Cecilia Chiang, of the restaurant Mandarin in San Francisco, frequently went to Taiwan. Would she bring back some fine oolong? Yes, indeed, in shopping bags stuffed with goodies for everyone. My tea arrived in its traditional packet: wrapped in a bamboo leaf tied at intervals. I tried not to look shocked when she told me the price. But it *was* a memorable tea, with many heady, light, mouth-caressing aftertastes.

I kept on shopping around for interesting teas, and, on a trip to New York, Marvin Rubenstein of *Tea Timers* magazine let me look in his files at his tiny office, and I found a letter from a retired Air Force captain in La Jolla who had a cousin in Germany who had a friend who worked in the Bunting Tea plant, where one of the world's finest Ostfriesen teas is blended. Far-flung Germans could order through him if they wished a taste of home; he would lean on his cousin, who would lean on the friend, and so on. I signed up in a second, bypassing the more expensive traditional route through a broker; and I could be sure it was from Bunting and not "a fine tea from that area that is just as good."

When friends went to India, I pleaded for the most expensive Darjeeling they could bring home, and anyone who went to London had to visit the Bramah Tea Museum and pick up some of Edward Bramah's superb Ceylon tea, an example of a short-leafed tea with an *outstanding* flavor.

In the packet, Mr. Bramah's tea looks like many a supermarket tea, tiny granules that will roll around in the palm of your hand. What a revelation to taste it and find that this tea (carefully supervised from garden to factory to ship) is one of the brightest ever. The adjective "brisk" takes on a new meaning.

I learned a lesson from the expression on Mr. Bramah's face of polite horror at my ignorance when I asked him if his tea was long-leafed. I was implying by my positive tone that if it was high-quality tea it naturally *had* to be long-leafed. (Long-leafed teas are usually finer, but not always.) A short-leafed tea properly processed—its oxidation perfectly timed and the sorting, shipping, and storing all in harmony—can be, in Mr. Bramah's words, "very close to heaven." His tea has the leaf grade of B.O.P., standing for Broken Orange Pekoe. Usually this means a sort of everyday tea, but this one is a wonderful exception.

Everything connected with the culture of tea fascinated me: the geography I was beginning to learn, the tea terms

B.O.P. stands for Broken Orange Pekoe. Broken means that small leaves have been cut up to promote flavor.

Orange refers to the

1. white downy tips of the emerging tea leaf;
2. orange blossoms layered into the tea before shipping—an obsolete, and perhaps apocryphal, technique of adulterating tea under the guise of providing flavor;
3. the Netherlands royal House of Orange (denoting a large leaf of high quality).

All are conjectures; take your pick.

F.T.G.O.P. stands for Fancy Tippy Golden Flowery Orange Pekoe. Tippy means the packet contains young leaves, and Golden means mature leaves are there, too. This is good technical information but gives not a clue as to taste.

In India and Ceylon, Pekoe and Orange Pekoe are the two largest leaves.

Pekoe is properly pronounced PECK-oh.

Thomas Lipton bought up a number of Ceylon tea estates in 1890, following the coffee blight there, and popularized the tea in England.

The spring blossoming of tea bushes in Ceylon is legendary—thousands of tiny white flowers giving forth the unparalleled fragrance of acres upon acres of roses.

Perhaps our tea language has been affected by this rose phenomenon: the Red Rose tea brand, the popular turn-of-the-century tea rose, and the roses decorating many a teapot and teacup.

from other languages that had worked their way into ours, the lore and history, the teapots and chinaware, the politics of agricultural economy in the developing nations. . . .

Another small triumph was the introduction of new teapots to the restaurant. We had been using sage green china pots that had a pretty shape and a certain humble charm, but when we started using new dishes from a local pottery, the teapots looked out of place. I wanted a new all-purpose pot that didn't look like cheap restaurant ware, that didn't drip, that didn't break easily, and that had a little class. With perfect timing, my dream teapots appeared in a neighborhood shop window. The owner had been born in Tokyo and couldn't resist offering these teapots from home for sale. They were low, round, humble, and cast iron. Their practical simplicity suggested a cozy hut with a wood-fire brazier deep in a Japanese pine forest with a small rustic temple nearby. Quiet serenity radiated from the nubbly black finish. I was nuts about them.

Establishing any change in procedure at Chez Panisse can be a little like demonstrating a tap dance in a lurching rowboat on the high seas on a foggy night, when the crew doesn't want to dance. Timing is everything. Sometimes a quick

---

Those initials on packets of tea are not much help when buying fine tea. They identify only the size of the leaf, not its quality.

In central China and in Taiwan the largest leaf is called Souchong. Lapsang is a made-up Western word that is meaningless in China. Possibly it is the Englishing of a word related to "mountain."

In the presence of confusing tea terms, remember Lu Yu's admonition: "Goodness is a decision for the mouth to make."

Be guided by the taste of tea, not by a fancy label. Buy what you like, and don't be shy about spending a little extra. Fine tea is always a bargain.

Many Japanese cast-iron teapots are now sold with a glassy finish on the inside; the old-fashioned unfinished cast-iron kind has to be wiped out after every use to retard rusting. Both have advantages.

Is gunpowder tea, often the first green tea a newcomer to tea will try, so-called because the tightly rolled pale greenish gray leaves rolled into tiny balls look like gunpowder? Or was the leaf considered to be the color of gunpowder? Another tea mystery.

The three basic categories of Japanese green teas are bancha (*partially made from branches*), sencha (*leafier and higher quality*), and tencha (*or macha*), *the ceremonial powdered tea.*

time-step in place is best, and sometimes a slow glide. Sometimes only steady bailing will do.

This time a quick rat-tat-tat time-step worked. I had selected five different teapots to choose from, and pulled up with them in my car just as Alice dashed by on foot. I collared her, whipped out the pots, put them on my trunk, and asked her to choose. "This one!" she said, putting her little mitt on my favorite. "It's great! Gotta go!"

And so we had new pots. They were an instant gotta-have-one success. But they had a drawback: unless wiped out right after use, they rusted. Another picky task the bussers wouldn't take time for! And since the pots weren't supposed to be put through the dishwashing machine, would the dishwashers take time to wash them out by hand—and dry them? Of course not. Mr. Peet and other professionals warned me it would never work, and for a time it didn't. The teapots were getting rusty. Then I figured out that if the pots were simply rinsed and stored upside down, they would dry out. The dishwashers graciously rinsed them, and on Sunday mornings I was there to stack them upside down in bus tubs, ready to go upstairs. I thought that if they saw me do it the right way the first time, they might get in the habit. I went around obsessively rearranging the shelved pots and joking about how cute they were.

After seven years of nudging, I walked into the café after a summer off, and there they were: every single one with its little bottom up. And the best accolade of all came from Mr. Samuel Humfrey Gaskell Twining, who graced our café one night for dinner. This ninth-generation tea merchant took one look at our iron teapots and blurted out, "Jolly good! Never seen these used before. How did you manage to keep the rust away? I say, do they really work?" I admit it—I was smug.

Around that time customers began to nudge us toward serving green teas. I didn't know it then, but I was at the kindergarten level of green tea knowledge. Dragon Well was the first one we served at the café, a safe beginner's choice. Then I branched out in all directions: first a humble Japanese *bancha,* a tea made from fresh stems and branches and a few leaves—a workingman's tea. Then a *sencha,* a cut above the bancha (literally, more leaf)—

clear, clean, and beautiful; everyone was enchanted with it when we served it at a dinner with Japanese dishes on the menu. But some of those who partook of it were up half the night, having assumed that green tea has no caffeine at all. Wrong!

One of my most ambitious failures was iced sencha. It has a nice little bite, it beautifully complements hearty food, and it is a perfect choice for those who don't want to drink boring sparkling water with their meal, but won't or can't drink wine. I made a concentrate, left it at the bar, and thought that it would be a great success. But if sencha is not drunk immediately it turns brackish. Wonderful choice for home use, but not for the restaurant. *Gen mai cha* ("brown rice tea") was a huge success, however. Made from sencha or a high-grade bancha (or any simple green tea) and cut with toasted brown rice, it is toasty, delicious, and flexible. Kids in Japan drink it the way our kids drink cocoa. When the ex-governor Jerry Brown came to the café with a Zen master plus entourage, I sent over some gen mai cha at the end of their meal. As they took the lids off the black pots to peek, the monks' stony faces—burnished and healthy from the sun, but so impassive during their meal—suddenly brightened and radiated pleasure. "Aah!" they said, in unison, "Gen mai cha!" Ever since, I have been particularly enthusiastic about this tea. Roy Fong now supplies us with a fine version made from organically grown tea and organically grown brown rice.

The man behind my new life at the restaurant is Peter, of the pepper toast tea party. A restaurant pro who grew up in Vienna, he is now the floor staff personnel manager. His attitude toward the work of a waiter is a world away from that of the American lad who decides to wait tables for a while until his life really begins. Peter believes things should be done "properly," a word he pronounces with that rippling, gutteral "r" sound that is so Viennese. Erect and precise, with a disarming, crisp smile, Peter will tell you softly that being late for work is "not very nice," and there is the ice of principle behind the smile and the understatement.

Peter keeps new bussers on probation for months before they are "hired." Then they are "allowed" to meet with me to be tea-trained. It is a rite of passage and a mark of their arrival. I congratulate them. They are alert, sensitive, and ea-

Do not judge the caffeine or taste potency of green tea by its color. Sencha is very pale, but has a fairly high caffeine content.

In Japan, if green tea is on the shelf for over two weeks, it's considered "dead" and either thrown away or sold at a tremendous discount.

ger to learn, and they ask wonderful questions. Because I've learned that handing an information sheet to a server about to go out on the floor is about as useful as handing him a restless pelican, I devised a tiny card that has the answers to the most frequently asked questions about our teas—about caffeine, where to find our teapots, how the peach tea is made, what teas take milk, and how long the teas must steep. Getting a tea card is now tantamount to being officially hired.

Now everyone at the restaurant seems genuinely interested in tea; I hope the teas—and the tea service—uphold the standard of Chez Panisse. For the best feedback I rely on two of my favorite chefs, Russell Moore and Richard Seibert, who have been interested in tea since the beginning. One likes highly tannic, astringent teas, the other low-caffeine soothing teas. They have been helping me select and taste for years.

Our downstairs chef, Jean-Pierre Moullé, happened to mention to me once that he drank a *tisane de verveine*—fresh lemon verbena leaves infused in hot water—every night before he went to bed. By an almost miraculous coincidence, that same week Alice started rhapsodizing about fresh herbal infusions, just as I was looking up how to pronounce *tisane* in English (the same as in French: tea-ZAHN). We began to offer them almost immediately. The gardens and farms of our suppliers were full of delicious herbs. I found some graceful glass pots from Belgium, devised a presentation with a thick white napkin folded under the pot, and soon the fragrant infusions were selling themselves. When a wonderfully aromatic pot wafted through the café, the customers would take a sniff and a look at the pretty green leaves floating inside—usually verbena or mint—and say, "I'll have one of those."

Some time later I had a cinematic moment of personal satisfaction when I was in the Manhattan office of *Gourmet* magazine's editor Zanne Zakroff. Her windows framed the spire of the Chrysler Building silhouetted against a sky of 1930s blue. I was feeling snitzy because an article I had written was going to be published. In passing, she said, "You're interested in tea, and you're from Berke-

> There is nothing at all mysterious about a tisane. Grab a small bunch of fresh herbs—lemon verbena or chamomile or mint—jam them in a teapot, preferably a glass one, and pour hot water over. The water doesn't have to be boiling. Make it as strong or as weak as you like.
>
> Some care should be exercised when buying dried herbs for tisanes. Yerba maté from South America has more caffeine than coffee. Mistletoe is poisonous.

ley. You must go to Chez Panisse and try their tisanes, and look at the pots. They're so gorgeous!" I restrained myself from jumping up and down and screaming, "That was me! Me! I found them!" I simply smiled and told her I had helped find the right pots. It was like a jigsaw puzzle when the last piece fits in with a little *click!*

And of course, for all my complaining, there have been a lot of little *clicks!* along the way. Customers who understand good tea (most of them from overseas) tell me that the tea at Chez Panisse is the first *real* tea they have had in an American restaurant. There are customers like the opera star who gushed that a particularly fragrant tisane was "the most *divine* beverage!" *Click!* And there are the locals who see me on the street and come up to me to confide that the reason they go to the café is for the peach tea. Not true, of course, but it is a lovely compliment.

But the compliment that most filled my heart came my way one afternoon in the narrow passageway in the downstairs kitchen. I had been trying valiantly, but unsuccessfully, to launch an exotic tea flavored with cardamom that I had called Egyptian tea. I was sure it would be a success; it was so good with ice cream. But people either love or hate cardamom, and the haters seemed to have had an edge. I withdrew it. But I got a soaring lift from Jean-Pierre. He was squeezing by with a tub filled with squid, and when he saw me he stopped and put it down. Turning toward me he made the classic cook's gesture for something tasty: thumb and first two fingers pinched together, pulsating in front of his pursed lips: "Ah, la belle Hélène! The Egyptian tea—it is a *beautiful* tea!" And another quiet but unforgettable moment flowed by.

RECIPES

Chez Panisse Lemon Tart

MAKES ONE 9-INCH TART

It was this tart, among other things, that first attracted Alice to the work of her partner and pastry chef, Lindsey Shere, before they launched Chez Panisse together in 1971. Along with David Goines, the poster artist, they had been working on a project for KPFA, a local noncommercial radio station. A dinner at David's and dessert at Lindsey's afterward was the beginning of a long-lived collaboration.

This is the same lemon tart you see on the bottom shelf of every Paris bakery display case. It is wonderful with Earl Grey tea, iced.

PASTRY:

1 cup flour	½ cup butter, room temperature
1 tablespoon sugar	1 tablespoon water
¼ teaspoon salt	1 teaspoon vanilla
¼ teaspoon grated lemon zest	

FILLING:

2 lemons	¼ teaspoon cornstarch
2 eggs, plus 3 egg yolks	3 tablespoons unsalted butter
6 tablespoons sugar	3 tablespoons salted butter
2 tablespoons milk	

To make the crust, mix together the flour, sugar, salt, and lemon zest in a bowl. Add the butter and mix with your fingers or a pastry cutter until the mixture re-

sembles coarse meal. Stir together the water and the vanilla, pour into the flour mixture, and mix just until the dough holds together in a ball. Wrap in plastic wrap and chill 30 minutes. Roll out the dough ¼-inch thick between two sheets of plastic wrap. Remove the top sheet and invert the dough into a 9-inch fluted tart pan. Peel away the remaining plastic wrap and press the dough into the pan. Trim the edges and place the tart in the freezer for 30 minutes or longer.

Preheat oven to 375°F. Place the chilled crust in the oven and bake for about 25 minutes or until the crust is a light golden brown.

To make the filling, grate the zest of the lemons into a small nonreactive bowl. Juice the lemons and strain the juice into the same bowl. In a heavy nonreactive saucepan, beat together the eggs, egg yolks, and sugar. In a small bowl, gradually whisk together the milk and the cornstarch, being careful to blend well so that there are no lumps left. Pour the milk and cornstarch into the egg mixture. Stir in the juice and zest. The mixture will look curdled, but will smooth out in the cooking.

Cut the butter in pieces and add to the saucepan. Over low to medium heat, stirring constantly, cook until the filling just coats the spoon and is the thickness of crème anglaise. Remove from the heat and let it stand 5 minutes to thicken, and then whisk lightly to smooth it. The filling can be made ahead and chilled.

When you are ready to finish the tart, preheat the oven to 375°F, spoon the filling into the prebaked tart shell, and spread it smooth. Place the tart in the oven and bake for 30 to 35 minutes, or until the filling is speckled with brown spots and puffed slightly. Cool on a rack.

Raspberry and Red Currant Tart (Clafoutis)

MAKES ONE 9-INCH TART

Of the hundreds of Chez Panisse desserts, I chose this one, mostly because when I thought about it my teeth started to hurt, a sure sign. The recipe was written out for me by Mary Jo Thoresen, a longtime pastry chef at the restaurant.

Part of the goodness of this tart comes from the pure fruity flavor of the unsugared berries.

PASTRY:

> 2½ ounces unsalted butter
> 2 tablespoons sugar
> 1 egg, room temperature
> 1 cup unbleached all-purpose flour

FILLING:

1 basket fresh raspberries	½ cup sugar
⅓ cup red currants, fresh or frozen	2 tablespoons all-purpose flour
1½ ounces unsalted butter	2 tablespoons ground blanched almonds
1 tablespoon milk	1 teaspoon framboise
1 egg, plus 1 egg white	

To make the pastry, cream the butter and sugar. Add the egg and mix until blended. Add the flour and mix until just blended. Form the dough into a ball and wrap tightly in plastic wrap. Chill for at least 2 hours, or overnight.

Roll out the pastry on a well-floured board and use it to line a 9-inch tart pan with a removable bottom. This pastry can be challenging to roll. If you rip or tear the pastry, simply patch it with some of the scraps. Save the rest of the scraps to patch any holes that may open up during baking. Place the tart shell in the freezer for at least 1 hour, or overnight.

Preheat the oven to 375°F. Place the frozen tart shell in the preheated oven and bake until light golden brown, 20 to 23 minutes. Check it about halfway through the baking and if the pastry is bubbling up a bit, poke it with a sharp knife to let the steam escape. Take the tart shell out of the oven and cool.

To fill and bake the tart, first patch any holes in the pastry with leftover scraps of dough. Pick over the raspberries and currants, discarding any bad ones. Place the fruit in the prebaked shell.

Put the butter and milk in a saucepan over medium heat. In a bowl, combine the egg, egg white, and sugar and beat at high speed until very light and fluffy. When the butter and milk mixture has come to a boil, remove it from the heat and slowly add it to the egg mixture while continuing to beat. When all the milk and butter is added, stop beating and gently fold in the flour, the ground almonds, and the framboise.

Pour this mixture over the fruit in the tart shell. Place the tart in the oven, still at 375°F, and bake for about 20 minutes. Turn the oven down to 325°F and continue baking about 15 minutes more, or until the center is set. Remove from the oven, cool, and serve.

Pepper Toast

On College Street in Calcutta, India, there used to be a tea shop called Basanta Cabin that served pepper toast to its British customers who requested a little something with their tea. (A good cup of Lapsang Souchong stands up to pepper toast.) Our pastry chef Lindsey Shere's husband, Charles, who is one of the founders of Chez Panisse, has always been a champion of this little treat. Here is his recipe word for word as it appears on a broadside calligraphed by Alice Waters and illustrated and printed by David Goines back in 1968:

"First, take two slices of good bread, whole or rye is best, & spread them thickly with butter. Then, liberally grind black pepper over each slice. Broil until golden brown, and eat hot."

Here is my version, which I prefer with tea: Toast slices of good-quality white bread, spread them with butter (no substitutions), sprinkle liberally with preground pepper from the pepper shaker, cut into triangles, and serve hot.

Chapter Eight

GENTLEMEN FARMERS ON THE PRAIRIE, OR THE SUMMER OF THE PEACH DUMPLINGS

In the middle of a perfectly ordinary Sunday morning in 1986, just as I was starting to do the dishes, the phone rang. It was a cousin telling us that the old Gustafson homestead was going up for auction. No one remaining from the original thirteen brothers and sisters wanted to buy it. "How about you guys?" he almost shouted. "Want to be farmers?" We'd always hankered after a farm, our Dakota and Nebraska roots happily entwining at last. Here was our chance. We said yes in our hearts in a heartbeat—but said yes legally a few weeks later after searching our pocketbooks and our prairie souls. Four months after that phone call we waded through the weeds and began prying open the windows, some of which had been sealed shut nearly as long as the house had been there, close to a hundred years.

It is an unremarkable old farm with nothing special about it except the spaciousness of its setting in the glacial lake region of the Dakotas, the same landscape Laura Ingalls Wilder made famous with her *Little House on the Prairie* books. And we are really only make-believe farmers. We rent out the fields to a neighbor to plant corn, winter wheat, and soybeans—and he fights Canadian

Growing all around our house, as they did around Laura Ingalls Wilder's little house on the prairie not far away, are wild prairie roses. Wilder loved them so much she named her only daughter, Rose, after them.

thistles. We visit in summer. In fact, we are jokingly referred to as the only summer people in the county. But standing in our yard under the stars we can feel the whole great prairie heaving and sighing beneath our feet and hear the rippling, soul-filling music of the crickets. And looking out across the expanse of meadow from the kitchen window and knowing that all we see is our very own, we have experienced something like perfect freedom.

We call the meadow to the west of the house the Dance Yard, to commemorate the impromptu victory dance we performed there the first day we spent on the farm. To the east are what we call the Piney Woods, after Winnie the Pooh, although there are no pines among the trees in the windbreak that runs alongside the road. The south yard is just called "the yard"; it borders the garages, the pig barn, the granary, and the big barn. The yard to the north is "out by the tea tree"; it contains a graceful old ash tree, and under it one sees the longest vistas and catches the sweetest breezes. This is the only spot on the farm that has never been plowed. The thin and pliant native prairie grasses still grow there and they ripple like waves on the ocean when the wind is right.

Time opens up on the farm. Each day takes on the aspect of two full days. There is time for everything, and there is everything to do. Baking, sewing, racing to the second-floor porch to catch the sunset at just the right moment or to watch the lightning prancing along the whole horizon. We also look for wild asparagus, have the neighbors drop in for tea, take in pie socials, watch the wild geese honk northward, chase Tramp Johnson's cows back into the pasture. . . . It's a full life.

For us the weather is remarkable, and we exclaim over thunderstorms like dogs yapping at a car window. But weather for the natives is a way of life. Wet and dry years, sudden hail the size of softballs, and killing heat are not things on TV—they relate to what one sits down to eat at the table. One day Bill and Bulah, our near neighbors, watched calmly as a tornado spun the fir trees out of the ground at the church just to the south, barreled up the "oil road," and, just as Bulah was moving toward the cellar, veered east to Tramp Johnson's windbreak and steel outbuildings. The funnel made toothpicks of the trees and crumpled the buildings like aluminum cans. Bill turned to Bulah: "I *knew* there was a good reason for not having trees up by the house. They catch the wind's attention."

On the sidewalk of many a midwestern town you will see a jar of clear pale liquid huddled against a sunny brick wall in front of the insurance office or in a south-facing corner at the gas station. Passersby step gingerly around it. It is sun tea, and this is how you make it: Fill a glass jar that holds a gallon or so with bottled cold spring water. Add tea bags or a favorite tea tied up in a piece of cheesecloth. Cover and put the jar in a sunny spot for two or three hours. Take out the tea bags, and refrigerate the jar before serving.

Moon tea is the overnight version of sun tea, but you don't have to set it out in the moonlight. Note that since neither sun tea nor moon tea has been boiled, it should not be kept for more than a day, as it tends to take on a fermented taste.

"Day tea" is my own impatient alternative to sun tea, and requires far less time. I simply use leftover tea of any kind, pour it into a glass, dilute it to the desired strength, and keep it by my side all day, replenishing as needed. Day tea is a lovely little tipple that can keep me on a pleasant roll for hours. (This is particularly true when I use green tea.) For those who dread drinking eight glasses of water a day, day tea, if sufficiently weak, is a happy substitute that will leave you feeling irrigated but not flooded.

Our neighborhood of fifteen families is south of the lake and covers about fifty square miles. The outermost farms belong to Erling (Tennie) Tenneboe, Sigvald and Sigrline Soderstrom, Pig Larson, and Royal Bjorklund. We have our own column of gossip and news in the bimonthly newspaper published in town (population: one thousand), just as if we were a real incorporated township. We have two churches, both small, white, and surrounded by spruce trees painstakingly nurtured with water hauled up from the lake so many years ago. The one to the north is Norwegian; the southern one is Swedish. The congregations mix now, but they didn't always; for years the county was divided by an invisible fence.

The second or third summer we lived on the farm I thought I should hang Japanese lanterns in the trees, hire the Old Swedish Fiddlers, and throw a neighborhood dancing party. There are no caterers, of course, but there are service clubs that put on the big lunches served at the daylong farm sales and auctions where two or three hundred people gather to bid on everything on a farm that can be carried off. You choose from among the Gabalots, the Du-Kums, or the Happy Homemakers. Much as I longed to give a party with the help of the Du-Kums, I backed down because I was afraid of making too big a splash and looking like a California show-off.

Both churches have their own service clubs as well, still known as Ladies' Aid. A different lady is chosen to "serve Aid" at each meeting, which means to serve the obligatory goodies after the business part of the meeting (praying, quilting, sewing, and so forth) is concluded. One of my aunt Bertha Gustafson's grandsons, when told that his grandmother had served Aid that week, thought this meant that she had surveyed her land—not really a farfetched idea, because Bertha can do most anything. Another grandson sneaked away from home to spy on a Wednesday afternoon ladies' meeting and discovered that the ladies were serving neither Kool-*Aid nor* lemon*ade!* A bitter blow.

Bertha lives about a mile northeast of us, in the oldest house in the neighborhood, built of stone with wood siding and with a second-story balcony we copied for our own farmhouse. She has acres of yard and a sheltering half circle of spruces, like the churches do. Exactly a quarter mile to the east are our closest neighbors, Bill and his missus, Bulah. One and a half miles west are Wilma and Herbert on their rolling hilltop farm. All three of these near neighbor ladies are grandmothers, and they know exactly how to make the same kinds of sweet things my Muttie made. Wilma's sugar cookies, with their daintily scalloped edges, are the best I have tasted anywhere, anytime. Herbert himself fashioned her cookie cutter, and she rolls them so thin you can almost read the newspaper through them.

Bulah's lemon meringue pie makes me put down my fork in pure amazement every summer: exquisite lemon filling, perfect meringue, spectacular crust. (It took me seven years to wangle the secret ingredient for that crust out of her.) Like many busy farm wives, Bulah is reluctant to commit to future social engagements; call her on Monday inviting her for tea on Wednesday and

Iced tea, it is said, was invented on a hot day at the 1904 Saint Louis World's Fair by the proprietor of a fancy tea pavilion. Seeing that his potential customers were passing him by, in a flash of inspiration he started brewing strong tea and pouring it over ice. Today 80 percent of all the tea consumed in the United States is iced tea.

she'll be evasive. But she doesn't want to disappoint the kids, as she calls us, so no matter how busy she is, she always finds time to have us over, usually on short notice, for a lemon pie dinner: complete with chicken, mashed potatoes and gravy, her own garden vegetables, renowned beet pickles, light-as-a-feather buns, and Jell-O salad. She will have bought a lemon in advance to have on hand for the pie, so she can be spontaneous with the invitation and avoid a wasteful ten-mile trip to town for just one item.

Bertha's truly old-fashioned date roll-ups are a rich, dense, and satisfying reminder of desserts of the past. The sweet natural flavor of the dates comes right through, not masked by too many spices, and reawakening my childhood memories of the simple cookies that Muttie made for teatime.

God must be rewarding me for something to have set me down smack dab in the midst of these benevolent baking angels to pursue my vision of farm life: a little work in the morning, then a change of clothes, and an afternoon devoted to sitting on the porch drinking iced tea or lemonade and eating sugar cookies while tatting or embroidering. The first year on the farm I decided I had to have all the neighbors for tea to repay them somehow. I set up an outdoor tea table near the Piney Woods, with cookies, iced tea, and lemonade. The tea was a success, but windy. I took a group photograph of the event, and every mouth was clamped shut in thin midwestern style. I took the hint and the next year I moved the tea *indoors,* to our civilized cool dining room with its oyster-colored wallpaper and lovely pale linoleum floor. Now I give this small tea party every summer.

It has been, since the very first time, a look-forward-to event, and planned ahead, in contrast to our usual drop-in style of socializing. I started calling it the Four Corner Tea, since each of us lives in a quarter section whose corners meet at the crossroads out by my west 40. Hand-lettered invitations are dropped into mailboxes from my open car (another red convertible, a '63 Comet). I get out my latest favorite tablecloth from one of the nearby "junktique" stores and purchase coordinating material for napkins, which I

Our favorite iced tea at home is the same kind my husband used to drink in his college days. He would come home from a hard day pouring concrete—his part-time job when he was an undergraduate—to a tall, glistening glass of iced tea his mother had set out for him, a thick slice of orange wedged in the midst of the ice cubes. That tea was Red Rose brand, from the A&P down the street, but any ordinary supermarket black tea will have the right mellow taste with an orange slice in it.

When iced tea becomes cloudy, add a little hot water to it, and it will become clear. The cloudiness does not affect the taste of iced tea.

fringe to one-quarter inch, in the old-fashioned way. (This lends precisely the right degree of *bon ton.*)

And the ladies dress up! Aunt Bertha is usually the first to arrive, in a stylish swirl, dressed in a black linen shirtwaist dress punctuated with a freshly pressed tatted handkerchief. She is a delight—those luminous bright brown eyes, that impish smile, and her perfect, naturally lustrous, bouncy gray curls. Next comes Wilma, tall and ash blond in immaculate sport clothes or a freshly ironed blouse and skirt. Her fingernails could be in an ad, they're so pristine, yet she is an active homemaker. Petite Bulah arrives always in a fancy knitted top and white slacks with touches of delicate jewelry positioned here and there. I throw on my farm dress, a cool cotton voile shift, and wear my sandals so I can rush around and not get too sweaty. We take photographs every year; and the dining room, with its high ceiling and fancy window moldings now painted dusty white, looks impressive, even dignified.

For my first teas I relied on cookies. In their own homes my neighbor ladies' fancy-cookie repertoire never ventured far beyond their own classics, which they were continually baking, and I noticed with a little pain that on drop-in visits to my place, they had all rather pointedly stayed silent when I had served them some of the foreign things we had happened to be eating: yogurt and a little fruit, or a slice of apple galette. I took the cue and stuck with cookies, which constitute one of the basic food groups in the Midwest. Bakeries in even the tiniest towns devote at least one display case—five feet long by four feet high, with three shelves—to nothing but cookies.

We always had cookies at our house when I was young. Mrs. Grout, my mother's mentor, declared she liked nothing better than a good substantial breakfast cookie. She made them, my mother made them, and that settled *that.* On midwestern farms in those days, substantial breakfast cookies were fodder for men's lunches out in the field. "Lunch" translated as "morning or afternoon snack" and included sandwiches, lemonade, cake, and sometimes doughnuts. (My favorite doughnut, flavored with applesauce, is smaller than most [needing less deep-fat frying time] and its moist tastiness is legend. My very beloved aunt Alverta was famous for them. They were "dainty," an important word in the thir-

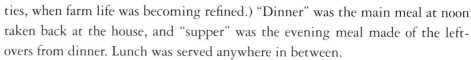

Switchel is the name for a thirst-quencher of a century and more ago, a combination of apple juice or vinegar, tea, ginger, sugar or molasses, and water—ingredients that were always at hand on the farm. Some herbal tea companies still make it; it's always good.

ties, when farm life was becoming refined.) "Dinner" was the main meal at noon taken back at the house, and "supper" was the evening meal made of the leftovers from dinner. Lunch was served anywhere in between.

Nowadays farmers ride in air-conditioned tractor cabs with well-stocked insulated coolers, but back then a young person from the household would hand-carry the cookies, sandwiches, and jugs of lemonade out to the fields. This same Aunt Alverta used to be assigned this job in the summer back in the twenties when a pale, "Beside-the-Shalimar" complexion was de rigueur. What a vision she must have been, her slim figure inching through the cornfield with lunch for the men, balancing her basket, hiding under a parasol, her arms and legs protected from the sun with sections of long white underwear. I still have an enchanting little photograph of her all in white, with just a few of her dark curls escaping from her sunbonnet.

I have made an unscientific but intensive study of cookies in our part of the Midwest and have come up with a list in order of popularity. First, of course, come sugar cookies—big ones!—just nosing out chocolate chip. Then oatmeal-raisin and peanut butter in third and fourth places, respectively, and in fifth place, the date- or raisin-filled cookie. Rumors fly about this last cookie, which is harder to find, and therefore the more prized and talked about, by everyone from farmers with shoulders wide as an ax handle to frail old ladies in the nursing home: "I hear Althea Thue does these real well . . . makes 'em twice a week for the big gas station up by Waterville."

For my Four Corner Tea, I decided to choose a cookie in the last category that would be ladylike and not a stretch for anyone's palate: Spice Tea Drops, a raisiny recipe from the Saint Paul's Evangelical Lutheran Church cookbook of Osceola, Nebraska. I had been attracted first by their name; after baking them once, I knew I was adding them to my short list of cookie classics. There are times when I will rise from my bed to make these, in order to set my world to rights. But they drew a lukewarm response from my neighbors. No one asked for the recipe. The next summer I regrouped.

In another old ten-cent country church cookbook I found a preparation called Last Minute Pudding. It must have been a popular dessert because it could be made instantly from the staples likely to be on hand on any midwestern farm. Heavy cream is poured *around,* not on, soda crackers in a soup plate; home-canned stewed fruit is spooned on top ("Run down cellar, honey, and fetch up some of those real good plums from last summer"); and on top of that, a dollop of sweetened whipped cream and a dab of homemade preserves or jelly—or, optionally, a pinch of coconut, right from the can. I loved the efficient and expedient quality of this recipe, and I could picture the scene of its invention: on a Sunday afternoon in the days before telephones, a wagon pulls into the farmyard, carrying a family of six from a neighboring farm; the Sunday layer cake is gone, its plate clean as a whistle, but no matter—Last Minute Pudding will be ready in ten minutes.

The other recipe I decided to make was for the sugar-and-orange-rind version of Mother's buttered cinnamon toast, a staple of our sun room teas long ago. The proportion is about half finely grated orange rind to half sugar, although Emerald Swenson, who shared the recipe with me one day as we were piecing quilts, told me that some prefer three parts sugar to one part orange rind. She went to a funeral with a gallon-size Schwann's ice cream bucket filled with the tiny triangles, passed it around the seated circle of mourners (that's our custom here), and watched for the gleam of recognition in the eyes of the older folks as they spotted an old childhood treat. "Not *one* left when I got the bucket back," she said proudly. I figured they would be perfect for my tea party. I made them and got addicted, as many do. The oven temperature and time is about the same as for cinnamon toast. (You can bake them at a lower temperature for a longer time, for more of a melba toast effect.)

At the Four Corner Tea, I served the pudding first, with just a hint of smugness, pretty sure of conjuring up the past. Two ladies put down their spoons—"Oof! I'm way too full!" and "We used to have that a *lot.*" A pause, and then Bulah put her hand to her head for just a second and closed her eyes. Her mouth was tight. She didn't say anything, but I was pretty sure I had triggered some painful memory of scarcity and privation in the dark days of the Great Depression. The sweet orange toast got a nod of recognition, nothing more. That Four Corners Tea was not a failure, exactly, but it was not a success, either.

The next summer my tea party menus were changed forever by a visit to a lo-

In the Midwest approximately one-third of the loose tea sold is green tea. Next to the large red Lipton boxes of black tea on the supermarket shelves, there are always a few of the dark green boxes of Lipton green tea. My pet theory is that where traditions are strong, old ladies still favor the tea their great-grandmothers drank. Black teas were first introduced into the United States in about 1828 and were often called "burnt teas." Until the 1880s, most of the tea that was consumed was green or oolong.

When you buy green tea, beware the look-alike box with the label that shouts "decaffeinated!" It is chemically treated. Stick with the box that says "Natural Green Tea"—it's much better for you.

The Mormon preference for low- or no-caffeine beverages boosts sales of green teas in Utah and neighboring states.

cal fair. On this auspicious rainy day, I stumbled upon two discoveries that were meant for each other: at an antique booth, I found an enamel pan, deep apple green with smart black edges, a true relic of the 1930s; and at one of the women's auxiliary booths, warm apple dumplings for sale. Crouched in my leaky convertible, eating warm dumplings with homemade vanilla ice cream and cinnamon sauce, with sips from a mug of slightly overbrewed green tea (purchased from another booth) providing just the right acidic contrast, I felt the thrill of a dessert epiphany. I would make dumplings for the Four Corners Tea—a tea party dessert the ladies would like: something familiar from the past that was mellow and filling.

It was late summer and peaches were in season, so I switched from the common apple to the luscious peach. That summer was forever after remembered as the Summer of the Peach Dumplings.

Dumpling dough is easy to roll out and fun to handle; it doesn't come apart when you fool with it, as pie dough tends to do. With pie crust, if you miss the crucial proportions of fat to flour to water, or knead or roll too long, the crust is ruined. Dumpling dough is much more forgiving. Filling peaches with a little honey or sugar and butter and cinnamon, and wrapping them up in dough and twisting the tops is a little like playing with clay or Play-Doh. The method is a breeze, and they look so pretty in a green Art Deco pan. And the baker can hover over them protectively as they bake, basting repeatedly with a simple syrup.

That year the Four Corner Tea was easy. I served iced tea and the familiar green tea, and the dumplings took center stage. The moment I saw the ladies nibble a bit and heard the silence that followed, I knew I had hit a grand slam. That moment of silence after a tableful of eaters takes those first few bites is the best compliment of all. They are concentrating. Bertha broke the spell: "These were what Mother made. . . . *So* nice, not so sharp as pie." Wilma joined in: "So nice and *warm!* Mmmm." Bulah just ate, bite after bite after bite. "And the peaches," Wilma went on. "They're so good this year. . . . Haven't had these for a *long* time. We always had cinnamon sauce at home, too, on the home place, I mean."

I breathed a big sigh of relief; at last I had given them something of the same comfort that they had given me over those previous summers. As any real hostess can tell you (although the great ones are never so blunt), giving *is* better than receiving. "Well!" said Wilma, "I'm *full!* It's cereal and eggs for my men tonight." And she smiled, knowing how well she feeds them 99 percent of the time. Bertha and Bulah sighed contentedly and started drifting toward the door. I followed, thinking how I would make the dumplings next time: maybe with a little fruit melange . . . should be just as good, maybe better. Their relaxed faces as they stopped for the ritual second good-byes on the front porch were better than any amount of citified air-kissing and hand-pumping and elaborate compliments could have been.

Bertha and Wilma got in the car, and as we hovered over the open car windows for the third set of good-byes, LaVerl from the gas station in town roared into the yard with his wife, LaDonna, in their 1910 Buick, refurbished for the big centennial parade in town the next week. "Want to try her out?" they shouted. Bertha and Wilma wanted to go home, but Bulah and I jumped in and I drove the quarter mile up to her house in style; she hunkered down in the not-yet-restored back and hung on as best she could. The car sputtered and jerked a bit going up the hill, but we made it to Bulah's just as the sun was setting and caught the breeze that follows sunset. The horizon glowed and the air was sweet and gracious. LaVerl and La Donna ambled up the hill, Bulah went inside to start supper, and I walked home thinking about giving and taking, tea and tea parties, and the good life, farm life.

South of the Mason-Dixon Line, iced tea is always sweetened, and often poured without charge in restaurants. Plain tea must be specially requested. Extravagant icing of the tall glasses and the promising tinkling of the cubes are hallmarks of the good Southern host. A sloping spacious white front porch is almost required.

Homemade cold tea punches flavored with additions such as fruit juices and spices still have a special place in Southern culture, although since the big beverage companies discovered an untapped market for this sort of thing, they have launched a thousand flavored tea drinks, canned and bottled, still and carbonated, oversweetened both naturally and artificially. They all contain some tea and are now available in every convenience store.

RECIPES

Wilma Haufschild's Sugar Cookies

MAKES 5 TO 6 DOZEN COOKIES

A scalloped 3-inch cookie cutter definitely improves the flavor of these cookies—as does a narrow counter and an open window that lets in sounds of ruminating cattle and shafts of late-afternoon sun. Watching Wilma roll and cut the dough with gracefulness that comes from performing a task hundreds of times gave me the courage to try it myself. Her calm voice sounds in my ear as I work: "Roll THIN!"

3 cups all-purpose flour	2 eggs, lightly beaten
½ teaspoon baking powder	1 cup sugar, plus extra for
½ teaspoon baking soda	sprinkling on cookies
½ pound salted butter	2 teaspoons vanilla extract

In a large bowl, sift together the flour, baking powder, and baking soda. Blend in the butter until mixture resembles very coarse cornmeal. Make a well in the center, add the eggs, 1 cup sugar, and the vanilla. Stir until the mixture forms a cohesive dough. Scoop the dough onto a large piece of plastic wrap and shape the dough into a log about 4 inches in diameter and 8 inches long. Wrap tightly and refrigerate at least 2 hours or overnight.

    Preheat the oven to 350°F. Unwrap the dough, put it on the counter, cut it into 4 equal pieces. Put 3 of the pieces back in the fridge and put the remaining 1 on a floured board with the long side facing you. Roll out the dough, making a trough. The dough should be no more than ⅛ inch thick in the center of the trough. With a floured cookie cutter, cut as many 3-inch cookies as you can from the thinnest part of the rolled-out dough, usually about 3 at a time. (This is the secret of Rolling Thin—only a few cookies are cut at a time so the thinness of the dough can be controlled.) Place them on an ungreased cookie sheet. Press the scraps back into a log and repeat until you've used up all the dough. It will become soft and hard to handle very quickly, so try to handle as little as possible. Repeat with the remaining 3 pieces of dough.

Sprinkle the cookies with sugar and bake 7 to 10 minutes in the preheated oven. Watch them closely toward the end of the baking. The edges should be set and just turning gold. (If you overbake the cookies and they turn a little brown, don't worry: they will still be very, very good.) Immediately remove to a cooling rack.

Bertha's Date Roll-Ups

MAKES 4 DOZEN COOKIES

This recipe, which can be traced back to an old Fannie Farmer Cookbook, *I now consider Bertha's property. These cookies always remind me of Bertha's bright brown eyes. A sackful of them can smooth a business transaction, spark a romance, or repair a marriage. And they are good unfrosted.*

COOKIES:

4 dozen pitted dates	½ cup sour cream
4 dozen large pieces of shelled walnuts	1¼ cups unbleached all-purpose flour
4 tablespoons butter, softened	¼ teaspoon salt
¾ cup light brown sugar	¼ teaspoon baking powder
1 egg	½ teaspoon baking soda

GLAZE:

6 tablespoons butter
1½ cups powdered sugar
½ teaspoon vanilla
About ¼ cup cold water

Slice each date almost in two, lengthwise, and stuff with a large piece of walnut.

Preheat the oven to 400°F. Beat the butter, slowly adding the sugar, and continue to beat until light and fluffy. Add the egg, beating thoroughly, and stir in the sour cream. In another bowl, combine the flour, salt, baking powder, and baking soda, and add gradually to the egg mixture, beating until smooth and well blended.

With your fingers, smudge some of the cookie dough around each stuffed date and place on an ungreased cookie sheet, leaving about one inch between cookies. (The dough will not make a smooth and even layer around the dates, so don't even try.) Bake the cookies 8 to 10 minutes, or until lightly golden around the edges. Remove from the oven and transfer to racks immediately before they get a chance to stick.

While the cookies are baking make the glaze. Heat the butter in a small saucepan until melted, swirling the pan, and keep cooking until the butter is lightly browned. Remove from the heat and stir in the powdered sugar. Stir in the vanilla and enough water to make a glaze. While the cookies are hot, spoon the glaze over them. As the cookies cool the glaze will harden.

Bulah's Spectacular Lemon Meringue Pie

MAKES ONE 8- OR 9-INCH PIE

When "done up right," as Bulah would say, this pie will be talked about for weeks.

CRUST:

> 1½ cups unbleached all-purpose flour
> A pinch of salt
> ½ cup Crisco
> 1 tablespoon Miracle Whip
> 4 tablespoons water

FILLING:

> 1 cup sugar
> 3 tablespoons cornstarch
> ¼ cup cold water
> 1 cup hot water

> ¼ cup lemon juice
> 1 teaspoon grated lemon zest
> 3 egg yolks, lightly beaten
> 2 tablespoons butter

MERINGUE:

> 3 egg whites
> ¼ teaspoon salt
> 3 tablespoons sugar
> 3 teaspoons water

To make the crust, first preheat the oven to 400°F.

Stir together the flour and salt, add the Crisco, and mix together with your fingers or a pastry blender until the mixture resembles coarse meal. Add the Miracle Whip and water and form the dough into a ball. Roll out the dough on a floured board to a diameter big enough to make an 8- or 9-inch pie. Line your pie dish with the dough, trim off the overhang, flute the edges, and prick the bottom of the crust all over with the tines of a fork. Press a sheet of heavy-duty foil over the pastry so that the crust will keep its shape when you bake it.

Bake for 10 minutes, remove the foil, and bake for 18 minutes more. The crust should be the color of pecans. Remove from the oven and let it cool.

To make the filling, measure out the sugar and cornstarch into a saucepan, add the cold water, and stir until smooth. Stir in the hot water and cook the mixture over medium heat, stirring constantly, until it is clear and has bubbles around the edge of the pan. Stir in the lemon juice and zest and cook 2 more minutes. Whisk some of this hot mixture into the egg yolks, and pour them into the saucepan that's holding the rest of the sugar mixture. Continue to cook the filling, stirring constantly, for another 2 minutes. Remove from the heat and stir in the butter. Cool completely.

Preheat oven to 375°F. Pour the cooled filling into the cooled pie shell. To make the meringue, beat the egg whites and salt until soft peaks form. Gradually add the sugar and water, continuing to beat very fast, until the egg whites are shiny and form stiff peaks. Mound the meringue onto the pie, making sure that it is spread out to the fluted edge. Put the pie in the oven long enough to brown the meringue, about 5 to 10 minutes. Take out and let cool. Refrigerate if not eaten right away, but serve at room temperature, if possible.

Peach Dumplings

MAKES 4 DUMPLINGS

From the many fruit dumpling recipes in church cookbooks, I've chosen Mrs. Victor Ram-berg's. Published in Minnesota in 1962, it appears in a bright yellow volume entitled Kitchen Treats: Our Best Recipes from Covenant Church Women of the Braham District Northwest Conference.

Slightly unripe peaches sweetened to taste are fine for this recipe, but tasteless, woody peaches are not. If the peaches are poor, substitute apples or a melange of berries. As well as making the surface glisten, frequent basting helps seal the dough packets so the peaches will steam. The dumplings don't have to be neat and tidy, so long as the peach is sealed inside.

1½ cups flour	4 peaches, halved, pitted, and,
2 teaspoons baking powder	if you prefer, peeled
A pinch of salt	2 tablespoons cinnamon
½ cup butter, plus 2 table-	1 tablespoon sugar
spoons for the honey syrup	⅔ cup clover honey
⅔ cup milk	1 cup water

Preheat the oven to 350°F. Grease a 9×13-inch, low-sided baking dish.

In a large bowl, mix together the flour, baking powder, and salt, lifting and tossing with your fingers or a fork. Cut the ½ cup butter into the flour mixture with two knives or a pastry blender until the mixture looks like coarse bread crumbs, or like stirred-up sand at the seashore. Add the milk and form the dough into a bowl. Do not knead.

Roll out the dough on a floured surface to form a large square about ¼ inch thick. Cut the dough into 4 squares and place 2 peach halves, one on top of the other, in the center of each square. Mix together the cinnamon and sugar and sprinkle a little on top of the peaches. Make a little package of dough around each peach, bringing the corners up to meet on top at the center. If there is excess dough at the apex where the corners meet, twist it into a little knob. Seal the edges together with fingertips moistened with water. With a metal spatula, place the dumplings in the greased baking dish.

In a small saucepan, heat the honey, water, and the remaining 2 tablespoons of butter just until the butter is melted. Pour about a third of this syrup over the dumplings. Put the baking dish on a rack in the center of the oven, and bake for 30 minutes, basting at least twice with the rest of the honey syrup. The dumplings are done when they are golden brown and crisp at the edges and when the peaches are tender enough to offer no resistance when pierced with a skewer. Serve warm with whipped cream—or better, with vanilla ice cream.

Applesauce Doughnuts

MAKES 84 SMALL DOUGHNUTS

After I finally overcame my fear of frying, I was surprised how easy these were to make.
Make sure you immerse these darlings in newly purchased, never-used-before vegetable oil.
These doughnuts turn a lovely light brown in a twinkling and disappear down the throat
just as fast.

2 eggs

1 cup sugar

2 tablespoons tasteless
    vegetable oil, plus about 1
    quart more for frying the
    doughnuts

1 cup sweetened applesauce

1 cup buttermilk

5 cups all-purpose flour

1 teaspoon salt

4¼ teaspoons baking powder

1 teaspoon baking soda

1 teaspoon nutmeg

½ teaspoon cinnamon

Confectioners' sugar

Beat the eggs and sugar until light, add the 2 tablespoons oil, the applesauce, and buttermilk, and beat until smooth. Mix together the flour, salt, baking powder, baking soda, and spices. Add to the egg mixture, beating until well blended. Cover and chill at least 2 hours or overnight.

When ready to fry doughnuts, heat about 1 quart of vegetable oil in a large heavy pot to 375°F.

On a floured board, spoon out about ⅓ of the doughnut batter, and pat it flat with floured hands, about ½-inch thick. Cut out rounds with a 1½- or 2-inch cookie cutter, and make the rounds into doughnuts by poking a hole into each one with a floured finger.

Drop the doughnuts into the hot oil and fry until light brown, turning once. Do not crowd the doughnuts by frying too many at a time, and make sure that your oil does not get too hot or too cold. Drain the doughnuts on paper towels, and sprinkle with confectioners' sugar just before serving. (Or shake the doughnuts in a paper bag with confectioners' sugar.)

Emerald Swenson's Swedish Orange Toasts

Preheat the oven to 350°F. Mix together 3 to 6 tablespoons of fresh, finely grated orange zest with the same amount of sugar. Butter 6 to 12 thin slices of good white bread, place them on a cookie sheet, and sprinkle the sugar and orange peel on top. Place the cookie sheet in the oven for about 10 minutes, or for crisper toasts, a little longer. Cut in triangles and serve. They are good warm, but they are still good after a few days if stored in an airtight container.

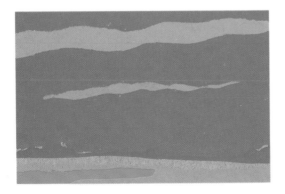

Mr. Twining's Iced Tea

Mr. Sam Twining's recipe for iced tea is just as he wrote it, and is, I believe, one of the nicest ever:

Use Twinings Ceylon Breakfast loose tea (because it is a high grown Ceylon tea) and put in one teaspoon more than you would normally use for hot tea. Make it in the normal way.

Put a small quantity of sugar at the bottom of a pitcher and fill it with ice. When the tea has brewed, strain the contents of the teapot over the ice.

As most teapots are smaller than pitchers, your pitcher is likely to end up about three-quarters full. Top it up with cold water, but do not garnish at this stage. Place the pitcher in the fridge until you are required to serve the tea, then garnish it with a slice of cucumber or lemon, bruised mint or borage leaf. It is the most more-ish [a Briticism related to "s'mores"] drink I know!

For tea drinkers who demand beautiful, fresh-tasting iced tea, brewing the tea extra strong allows for a moderate amount of ice to be present without diluting the tea. Pouring hot tea over ice cubes produces a weak, half-hearted warmish drink that does not satisfy the true tea drinker. Another trick is to make ice cubes out of the same kind of tea. Then you can use all the ice cubes you want without them diluting the drink as they melt.

Chapter Nine

TEA WITH MR. T.

After my golden hour drinking Twinings Two Hundred Seventy-fifth Anniversary black Yunnan tea with Camille, I never stopped wanting more of it. I stashed dozens of the square scarlet tins, which reminded me of British telephone booths, but finally all were emptied. Would the Twining company ever supply us again with this warm, peaceable tea, so benign it required no milk? The Anniversary blend was an encouraging tea, with no threat of an afterbite—that dread, bitter punch to the tummy that a black tea sometimes gives. Its golden twisted leaves conjured up fantasies of soft, sunny days romping with cousins in a meadow near the sheltering oaks of a big manor house. I was devoted for life to this tea; I was besotted with it. It made me feel secure, and it improved my digestion.

Fired up, I wrote to the company's American representatives in New Jersey. No answer. Time passed. Then when I began to plan a long-awaited vacation to the Lake District, the idea occurred to me of visiting Mr. Twining himself. Letters danced back and forth across the Atlantic. My first request for an interview went unanswered. To my second letter, I received a two-line reply ending:

The province of Yunnan in south central China is believed to be the birthplace of the tea plant, Camellia sinensis. On the other side of the Himalayas, in India, grows another wild tea, the variant called assamica. Starting about 1856, the China tea was planted in Darjeeling, in northern India. The rest of the tea of that country and several other tea-growing areas derive from what is known in the tea trade as assamica jat (the local name of the bush that flourishes in Assam).

"Mr. Twining regrets he will be in Sweden during the time that you will be here." I wrote my third letter on Chez Panisse stationery, without alluding to my previous letters, and was rewarded with a fat envelope with an engraved return address surmounted by a tiny gilded crest: the royal arms with the legend beneath explaining Twinings is "By Appointment." Inside was a two-page letter granting my wish and concluding with this telling sentence: "If you will but let us know the time of your arrival, a driver will meet you at the station and bring you to the factory for an interview, lunch, and a tour with Mr. Twining." I loved the "but"—how British!

Perhaps I stood a chance of persuading the company to sell the Anniversary Yunnan again. Perhaps I would receive a heroine's welcome as its foremost American champion: a roomful of elegantly dressed tea buyers at auction would leap to their feet to applaud my modest entrance. I had seen photographs of modern tea auctions: an austere room, gray-haired gentlemen all looking straight ahead. Quite dignified and solemn, and not at all like the old London tea auctions in the Plantation House rotunda, with its grand Georgian decor, all polished wood and brass, and a dome from which light streamed down upon the noisy top-hatted buyers below. I imagined a scene like that of the House of Commons—brawling, yet civil. Surely modern tea auctions must retain some of that elegance and vigor.

When I arrived in London, I phoned Mr. Twining's office to confirm my interview and ask if it could be arranged for me to witness an actual auction. I gathered this was not the usual thing, but my tourist's insouciance was re-

*Porcelain from China—
chinaware—was
imported to England by
ships' captains, who were
allowed to fill the empty
places in their ships' holds
with it; they later sold it for
their own profit.*

*In the days of the clipper
ships, the voyage from
Canton to England took
about one hundred days.
Amazingly, fine teas today
take just about the same
amount of time to reach the
consumer. The tea that ends
up in tea bags has been
traveling about three months
by the time it reaches your
cup at home.*

warded. Indeed, yes, I might attend an auction the very next day. I need but report to Mr. Dominic Beddard, tea broker with Wilson, Smithett & Co., at his offices in Sir John Lyon House, the home of the National Tea Council and the site of the auctions, where millions of pounds of tea are sold every year.

On the appointed morning, I rose early so as to arrive at Sir John Lyon House promptly—the auction was to begin at 10:30. It was a raw, grim, rainy day in early spring; the air was tense with the changing season. Sir John Lyon House is just off Upper Thames Street, running close and parallel to the banks of the Thames, where many old tea businesses are still located. In the old days, tea was first unloaded nearby just below Tower Bridge at St. Catherine Dock. The street names in that neighborhood make me ache to see it as it was then: Cathay Street, Teak Close, Mandarin Stairs, Cinnamon Street. When these streets were at the center of the China trade, they had echoed with bustle and energy. Here spices, porcelain, and chests upon chests of tea were unloaded—the tea probed by testers watchful for adulterants, such as ash leaves, extra quantities of jasmine flowers, even sheep's dung, that were sometimes added to boost the weight of the chests. Then the tea was brought to the neighborhood of Plantation House, to be auctioned and sold on Mincing Lane. Three days later, the same tea had been delivered by coach as far away as Scotland.

Upper Thames Street today, still home to the tea trade, is not like the cheerful Fleet Street of the newspapers farther to the west. It is grimy, industrial, and *old*. A cobblestoned passageway led me to a courtyard surrounded by somber stone buildings that looked like workhouses. I knew that one of them was Lyon House, but I could see no numbers or signs. Alleyways led down to cement-walled dead ends; stairs led up to bricked-up doors. I was going to be late. Nothing seemed to correspond to the directions I had been given. My ankles were hurting. I picked out another building at random and climbed another flight of stairs to a nondescript black door. A tiny plaque told me I had chosen the right one. I entered.

The inside of Sir John Lyon House suggested nothing so much as a dreary, underfunded elementary school in the North of England: narrow halls, black-and-gray linoleum floors, and much-used bulletin boards everywhere. There was a ubiquitous, repellent odor of a badly vented institutional cafeteria. In the hallways I walked past restaurant-style tea carts on which sat many tea bowls, the kind known as tasters' cups, their lids filled with damp tea leaves. I leaned over to smell the leaves. That helped a little, but as I climbed to Mr. Beddard's office on the fourth floor, my spirits were wilting. The entry room was small, dark, and dusty. Tea tins were scattered on half-empty shelves. A door sprang open, and a very neat and down-to-earth secretary ushered me into a second room.

I began to revive, for the wall opposite me had a large window with a commanding view of the Thames. I walked over, looked down, and realized that a new wing had been built which projected over the water—the benevolent gray strength of that famous river flowed directly beneath my feet. I took a deep breath. There, just across this handsome river, had stood the old Globe Theatre. Nearby, Johnson and Boswell had embarked on a romp early one morning and rowed themselves to Kew. I found myself hoping Mr. Beddard would be late so I could have the river to myself for a while. As I waited, the sky began to change from dull gray to a blue gray shot with yellow-and-white clouds—a Turner sky. The spires of the city came to life. The whole scene had the spaciousness and grandeur that belong to London alone.

A door behind me opened and in bounded Mr. Dominic Beddard. He was blue-eyed and stiff-collared, his compact physique beautifully dressed and bristling with energy. Mother would have said that he was "pretty well fastened together." He rubbed his hands briskly and joined me at the window: "Ah, yes, a good auction day. We have high hopes! How *do* you do, Mrs. Gustafson? Do come this way!" And we were off, quickstepping down hallways, riding one elevator down and another up, striding across a covered pedestrian passageway high above Fleet Street. There, in another building, we were greeted by discreet security, identified, and given badges and green paper catalogs listing the tea to be sold that day. Then we were waved through two black swinging doors, and into a dimly lit room. The walls were curtained in dark gray. Long tables covered with grim cloths faced a small podium. Behind it, lights resembling huge car headlights glowed straight at us. The effect was almost hypnotic. We took one of the rear tables. I quickly counted about forty male heads. Although no one wore a top hat or a morning coat, everyone was dressed conservatively in well-tailored business suits of black or gray—not one blue or brown suit to be seen. I could make out every word of the murmur that rose from the front row; the acoustics were perfect.

The auctioneer entered swiftly and seated himself at his podium on which he placed a tiny gavel. Then he held up his fountain pen in front of him, as if he were an eye doctor checking our ability to focus. Next he picked up the gavel and said, with no further preamble, "Let's begin with Lot Number 403. May I have a starting bid?"

A pause, and then a quiet voice from the center of the room: "One hundred and thirty-five pounds."

"I am sorry, sir, but I can't start at that figure. This is a rather nice tea." (This was said in the quiet, even tone one might use to a restless child in church: "No, dear, now we sit still and listen to the man.")

A bid of one hundred forty-five pounds came from somewhere in the back.

"Thank you, sir," replied the auctioneer, holding his gavel by its head and using its handle like a pointer. His tone was eerily undramatic.

As if a sluice gate had opened, the bids, in low, controlled voices, began to flow. They continued without stopping. As the voices swirled around my ears, I looked at Mr. Beddard and mouthed, "Wow!" but he just gave me a quick nod and returned to his catalog, in which he was recording each sale.

All the bids were made in quiet voices, but I detected in some a note of challenge, in others a sense of embarrassment, and in still others a cool, remote formality. The heads of the bidders never turned. At the end the auctioneer flipped the gavel and brought the head down deftly from a height of all of six inches. It made a little click.

Lot followed lot and the tension grew as hundreds of thousands of pounds changed hands. The auctioneer smoothly set the tempo of the auction as if the bidders and their rhythmic jargon were the voices of an orchestra.

"Meet you at two, sir?" said the auctioneer, inclining the handle of his gavel in the direction of a bidder.

A disembodied voice in the rear answered, "Three?"

"That's a tempter," said the auctioneer, gesturing toward one of the bidders, a huge man to my left with a heavy thatch of gray hair that stood almost straight up. A pause. "No?"

I whispered to Mr. Beddard, "Who is this giant?"

"Brooke Bond Company, the biggest here today," he returned in a whisper. So this was one of the big Beverage Boys I had heard about. And he *was* a giant! After another pause, the big boy responded: "Four!"

"Thanks, Brooke's," said the auctioneer, a hint of gratitude in his voice.

The teas must have been getting better. Bidding for the next lot went just the same way, with Brooke Bond coming in for the kill at the end. This time the auctioneer ended the sale by saying, "*All* right, sir," in a tone that seemed to mean, "Okay, okay, you win." Or perhaps he was trying to coax Brooke Bond to bid higher on the next round.

On it went, relentlessly. I had to remind myself to breathe in between bids. Then the auctioneer surprised me with a new query, delivered in a lighter, flirtatious tone: "How much can you give me for this *Laura* lot?" *Laura* was the name of a ship. The lot must have been from a desirable estate; the room became more animated. Heads actually turned to one another and I heard a little rustling for the first time in an hour. When the bidding slowed down, the auctioneer said, "Pack it up, pack it up!" Brooke Bond had won again.

At one point I whispered to Mr. Beddard, "So *much* tea, but this is all ordinary supermarket tea bag tea, isn't it?"

He hissed back, "Yes, it all has to fit into that wretched little bag." He grimaced. His lot was coming up and he couldn't elaborate, but I was sure that he felt a certain contempt for the mass-market tea he was dealing in. Actually, larger, medium, and small teas are all sold at the same auction, with tea bag tea accounting for about 60 percent of the sales.

The auctioneer egged them on in his slippery voice of authority: "Any more to go? Any more to go?" The bids were coming in higher and higher, and for the

*T*ea is graded according to size. The biggest leaves generally yield the finest and most complex flavors (for Darjeelings, for example, and some well-known China teas). The biggest and longest leaves are called Pekoe and Orange Pekoe and contain a substantial amount of new-growth leaves and buds. In descending order the other main grades are Broken Orange Pekoe, Fannings, and Dust. Pekoe Fannings and Dust (so-called because they were blown away by the winnowing machinery in olden days) are the smallest primary grades, and are necessary to give the tea bag blends strength and color. Tea bag supporters insist that smaller grades are not inferior, only stronger, infusing more quickly than whole leaves.

first time I heard a mutter of discontent rising from the floor. The auctioneer paused, and said with a half-smile and the hint of a shrug, "I'm not *doing* anything, gentlemen," implying that it was not his fault if bidders chose to bid against each other. A polite little laugh floated up from the room, relieving the tension a little.

Off to my right I noticed a younger man seated against the wall. He had a slightly windblown look, and unlike the others, he was wearing a tweed sport coat and slacks—gray, of course, but without the Savile Row elegance of all the suits. When the next lot came up and the giant from Brooke Bond began to bid, the young man softly called out, "Brooke Bond, please." Mr. Beddard volunteered an explanation: the young man was piggybacking his bid along with Brooke Bond's. Big Brooke didn't turn, but nodded curtly.

The bidding was more focused than ever, and the offers climbed higher and higher. Everyone's concentration was intense. I was flagging and hoped that we were near the end. The young piggybacking bidder was shifting in his chair uneasily. After another bid or two, he murmured, "Thank you" to no one in particular, and sank back against the wall. Mr. Beddard made a gesture of dismissal. Evidently the young man had withdrawn after riding along as far as he could. He looked miserable.

Scanning the room during the next lot, I was struck by the sight of a patch of brilliant jade green in the front row. It was a silk blouse; its owner must have removed her jacket. I nudged Mr. Beddard and pointed. "Yes," he replied, "a new phenomenon, just this year." She and I were the only women in the room. Like the man in tweed, she was piggybacking her bids on Brooke Bond's, and like the unfortunate young man, she had to get off. We heard her "Thank you," although Big Brooke went right on bidding, of course, and closed the sale. The silence that followed as people checked their catalogs was broken by Brooke Bond, who leaned back and, in a warm, condescending tone, said, "Sorry, love." My eyes popped open and I felt a cold shudder pass through the room. At least I hoped I had, and that it wasn't just a projection of my own revulsion. No time to speak of it to Mr. Beddard, who was deep in his catalog because his lot was almost up. And, to my shame, I never did.

The tweedy young man rose to his feet in confusion and sank down again; the auction was not over. Mr. Beddard entered the bidding. His demeanor was cool and elegant, and he seemed pleased with the results. There was a crisp "Thank you very much" from the podium and the auction ended. Everyone began to get up. I caught the eye of the young man in tweed, who raised his eyebrows and shrugged, as if to say, "Well, that's how it goes." But I could imagine what lay ahead for him: a humiliating conference with his boss and a miserable homecoming to his wife. I looked the other way and saw big Brooke stand up to his full six and a half feet. He was more rumpled than most of the other brokers and more at ease, and he had the expansive gestures of a professional athlete. I hated him.

We stepped out into the hallway, where bright, fierce morning light streamed through the windows. It hurt my eyes. The auction had lasted about an hour and a half.

I was thirsty, sweaty, and exhausted. The other men from Mr. Beddard's firm gathered around like a polite posse after a successful ambush. Rather than exchange high fives, they all shook hands. "Jolly good fun," said one. "Rather a good game, don't you think?" said another. I didn't think so, and said so: I thought it had been very serious, very fast, and very manipulated. "Well, no one's job depends on it, you know," he answered genially, without acknowledging my point, and turned away before I could respond, perhaps having dismissed me as a foolish woman and a sentimentalist. The mutual congratulations continued. It was beginning to sound too much like a postgame locker room wrap-up. But the auction had not been a game: it was a serious business.

We talked polite tea talk for a bit, and then I said my good-byes and thank yous and found a snug taxi to return me to my little hotel. I changed out of my sweaty clothes, stretched out, stared at the ceiling, and tried to sort it all out. This was not *my* tea world. This was its fiercely competitive underside, a nether world of garish trade magazines printed on heavy glossy paper, full of ads for tea bag paper and tea bag–making machines, and illustrated with photographs of businessmen with bad haircuts smiling stiff, industrial smiles: The Beverage Boys.

Yet it was rather bracing to realize that all was not intimate romance and quirky eccentricity in the world of tea. After the realities of the auction room, I expected my visit to the Twinings factory operation in Hampshire to reveal more hard truths. After all, I was about to visit a modern factory in rural England, not a tea garden in the foothills of the Himalayas, a factory that blends and packages tea and ships it all over the world.

I lay there, still perusing the catalog. On its back page was a list of all the gardens whose teas had been in the lots that day—all African estates. I read them aloud: Mettarora, Michi, Mini Mini, and Mogogo; Mulindi, Musongi, and Shagasha. They made a melodious chant. Looking through the catalog again, I read the names of the ships whose holds were crammed with tea. I knew they were probably ugly container ships, but their names were redolent with maritime romance and adventure: the sturdy-sounding CMB *Ensign,* the *Victoria Bay,* the *Earl Trader* (Earl Grey, perhaps?), the *African Star,* "lying in Port Saint Louis." For centuries, ships with names like these had lain in harbor, after making their way to London laden with tea from exotic climes. For centuries, the shoes of tea traders had worn down the cobblestones outside Lyon House. When the trade in tea was new, cavaliers in plumed hats strode the quays.

There was still elegance in the tea trade. I remembered the auctioneer smoothly overseeing transactions in the hushed room. And there was Mr. Dominic Beddard, perfectly dressed, gliding through it all. There is a grubby business side to the tea world, and probably always has been, but the romance is never far away.

ⓐ   ⓐ   ⓐ

The morning of my trip to the factory was as grim and wet as the morning of the auction had been. I dressed for the occasion in a high-visibility scarlet British sweater and the sort of heavy brogans that can tour all day, and I brought along a sturdy bag packed with notebooks, dress shoes, a snack, and a big bottle of water. I felt like a foreign correspondent. The train ride from London was peaceful. I rather hoped the driver who was to meet me would be dressed like an Edwardian gamekeeper and be standing beside a vintage Bentley with his cap in his hand. However, the neat little man who greeted me at Andover Station was dressed in virgin polyester, circa 1990, and he was standing by a nondescript late-model sedan. He wore a traditional cap, but it was nylon, not Harris tweed, and it stayed on his head. He introduced himself as Joseph. Despite my disappointment, I allowed myself to hope that a luxurious motorcar ride still lay ahead during my day in Hampshire; after all, I had learned from his secretary that Mr. Twining himself was to drive me to our private lunch at a country inn. A Daimler would do.

Joseph drove me efficiently through some pleasant open country and through a small town. We then drove into what at first appeared to be another small town and finally down the long circular drive that led to what looked like a railway station. We stopped and Joseph let me out. The "station" was the heart of the tea factory itself. Buildings were set amid sweeping green open spaces, and scores of truck containers packed with tea sat rank on rank. I tried not to look rattled, but I was.

We marched up to a comfortably proportioned white concrete building in the efficient institutional style of the 1960s. Inside, I was reminded again of a school, but this one was prosperous. The glass cases in the reception area contained unusual teacups and teapots and documents from over a quarter of a millennium in the tea trade. Glancing at the clock, I saw I was five minutes early. Joseph told me that Mr. Twining would soon be down, and left. Sure enough, at exactly ten o'clock, a door on the mezzanine opened and a tall, well-proportioned man walked easily down the stairs. He wore the obligatory impeccably tailored gray suit, which matched a shock of gray hair combed to one side in casual schoolboy style. His eyes twinkled and he had a face with the kind of built-in smile that might light up any moment. I liked him on the instant. We climbed the stairs to his pleasant but by no means luxurious office.

I settled into a leather chair and Mr. Twining started the interview, speaking with the calm assurance of a practiced C.E.O. who had all the time in the world for me. He related the history of his forebears, weavers in Gloucestershire before they became tea men. One of them, Thomas Twining, bought an existing coffeehouse in 1706, just off the Strand, and began to specialize in quality tea.

*T*ea *was an extremely
expensive commodity in
the* 1700s, *costing as much
as eleven hundred dollars
per pound in present-day
currency.*

Later, in 1717, he purchased three small houses and opened the first tea and coffee shops in the Western world, "at the sign of the Golden Lion." Mr. Twining closed the coffeehouse when such places went out of fashion. One difficulty had been that no *lady* would be caught dead stepping in or stepping out of one of those male bastions. But at the Twinings tea shop, ladies could leave their sedan chairs and enjoy the conviviality that his sample cups provided. Tea became fashionable, the trade flourished, and Twinings eventually was purveying tea to the royal family, to archbishops and lords, and to such luminaries of the age as Alexander Pope and Dr. Johnson. To this day, Twinings maintains a shop at the original location, although the eighteenth-century houses are now wedged between much larger, later buildings. The doorway's graceful Georgian arch is still crowned with a gilded lion. And it is still a freehold property, so that, according to the present Mr. Twining, "Even if the Queen herself wanted it, she could not command it."

Mr. Twining continued the story of his family's fortunes in tones that suggested generations of authority. Feeling a little cornered by history, I suddenly heard myself blurting out, "This is all so interesting, but when do we get to gossip?" He fell for my sporty, big American smile, and we had a delicious go-round sharing human news of tea people we knew in common. Soon it was time for Syd to be rung for and introduced: Syd was to show me through the factory. Mr. Twining nodded affectionately toward the vigorous-looking, mutton-chopped, well-built man who appeared in the doorway. "Syd started work with us at age fifteen as a potboy; we were potboys together. You are in excellent hands, Mrs. Gustafson. Syd knows everything. No one knows it better.

"Do be back by eleven forty-five sharp, Syd, so that I may take Mrs. Gustafson to lunch!" This was delivered in solemn tones; Syd might as well have been tapped on the shoulder with a sword. The explosive "-ch!" at the end of this sentence made our lunch ahead sound very important and glamorous.

Syd was a man focused on details, and he was determined that I get my share of them. The details of the factory goings-on were dizzying: the enormous numbers of bags per hour, bags per day, bags per year. From an overhead catwalk we viewed row on row of tea bag–making machines, tended in an offhand way by a very few workers. The sheer quantities of tea bags, and boxes and cartons of tea bags, were almost unbelievable.

Then we climbed up many stairs to a windowless warehouse as big as a barn that contained a machine much like a grain elevator on the farm. And the atmosphere around it reminded me of a grain elevator in August: the tension in the air, the bustling workers, and the dust everywhere. This was the contraption that blends Twinings' best-selling tea, Earl Grey, twenty-four hours a day, 365 days a year. It sat there, about eighteen feet high and perhaps fifteen feet wide, with its four funnels making it look as if it had just touched down from space, roaring and throbbing and thwacking away like a marvelous cartoon machine. Free-wheeled hoppers looking like small open boxcars filled the room, each one piled high with a ton of Earl Grey. A ton of tea in a hopper is about the size of a minivan; brewed, a ton makes over half a million cups. And Twinings sells over ten million pounds of Earl Grey every year.

An old tea trade story, quite undocumented, has it that the famous recipe for Earl Grey tea was given in about 1835 to the second Earl Grey, a diplomat, by a grateful mandarin whose son's head the Earl had somehow saved from the chopping block. The tea, flavored with oil of bergamot (a flavoring not popular then or now in China), is supposed to have been first brought to Jackson's of Piccadilly, probably because it was the earl's neighborhood tea shop. But Twinings also claims credit for introducing it. Of course, today every tea company blends its own Earl Grey; some use lavender instead of bergamot. (I wonder if the Earl would have been pleased to know that even as a household word, he would retain both title and capitalized name: we wear cardigans and eat sandwiches, but we drink "Earl Grey.")

Bergamot is a variety of citrus fruit. It looks like a cross between a lemon and a grapefruit, and its skin, crushed, exudes an extremely aromatic oil. Added in very small amounts to black tea, bergamot oil acts rather like instant lemon—my theory is that when we add lemon to tea, we do so almost instinctively, to be good to ourselves.

When we left the Earl Grey warehouse, I could sense that Syd was coming to a part of the tour he relished: the tea tasters' room, his old stomping grounds.

Twinings' annual production of Earl Grey tea is enough to fill four football fields to a depth of five feet!

A recent study done at the University of Wisconsin suggests that adding lemon increases the body's absorption of the calcium and iron in tea.

The room was large, pale yellow, and filled with light, overlooking green fields and the yards of the factory. Bordering the tasting room all-around were the little glass-walled offices of the tea tasters (five in all). In the middle were long tables with curious ledges bound in metal. On top of the tables was a row of testing cups (white lidded bowls like the ones I had seen at Wilson, Smithett)—thirty-six in all, I later learned. And in the very center of the room was an island of burning gas rings on which, steaming away, sat several remarkable cone-shaped copper tea kettles. I badly wanted one of these lovely large kettles. Three wholesome-looking, red-cheeked ladies were in charge of them; they propelled themselves around as if on roller skates, catching the kettles at the moment of the boil, pouring them down the long lines of cups with amazing deftness and speed, and then refilling them with fresh water and replacing them on the fire. When the kettles began to boil again they must have made a sound I couldn't hear, because the tea ladies would interrupt whatever they were doing and dash over to grab the kettles once more. Benign, sweet Mistress Quicklys, all of them.

The tasters at the tables would take a sip, inhaling the triple-strength tea over their tongues and making a loud slurping sound just like the one your mother taught you *not* to make. Then they would spit out the liquid into what I now recognized were mobile spittoons looking very much like gutters attached to the edge of the tables, flowing continuously with water; the old-fashioned spittoons had disappeared.

During my visit the Earl Grey was being tasted to confirm that the batch being shipped tasted exactly the same as always. The procedure is to taste the standard first, made in four cups, and then the new blends in the other thirty-two cups—all in one batch, by one taster. The department is sectionalized, each taster being responsible for a certain tea-growing area. Tasters do this kind of thing for hours at a time, day after day. For some drinkers, tea stains on their teeth can be a problem. I took a chance and asked Syd a personal question: "How often do you have your teeth cleaned?"

"Once a month." He grinned. He seemed to like my effrontery.

I asked Syd more about blending: How do you maintain quality so that a blend tastes the same year after year? In any region, teas must vary from season to season. A blend of Chinese teas from Anhui province, Twinings China Black, in its pretty baby blue box, had long been a favorite of mine. Recently, it had seemed not quite as wonderful as before. Was there a reason? A bad harvest?

"Oh, it has to taste the same," said Syd. "You must be mistaken." He pointed to an ordinary-looking man in the far corner. "That's Roy. He's been blending the China Black for more than thirty years." I was flabbergasted. Just this one man? The one who looks like my postman? How does he do it? I had envisioned whole committees of blenders, boardrooms full of blenders.

Syd steered me briskly into a room lined with shelves. The ones on the right wall held hundreds of brightly colored boxes of commercially available teas, from major tea-producing countries all over the world. On the left wall were boxes with carefully hand-numbered labels. These were specimens of specific teas used as benchmark exemplars. On the back wall were boxes containing numbered, folded pieces of heavy paper. These held handwritten formulas for matching the benchmark sample's qualities with different combinations of tea, and sometimes eighteen to twenty-five different teas are required to duplicate one of the samples.

If you needed to blend a batch of China Black, and one of the teas from Anhui wasn't quite right, you just looked up the right formula to duplicate the taste of the missing element. This system relies on the gardens to be consistent as well. I asked Syd how one can be sure that a garden will come up with the required quality. He replied, "Well, of course the estate manager at the garden is responsible for the quality of the tea manufactured. If his standards drop, his teas will receive lower prices at auction." But he made a discreet throat-cutting gesture.

It was time for lunch and I was hungry. I rejoined Mr. Twining and together we set forth in his car on twisting lanes to a nearby inn. The sun had come out again, the trees in the forest were budding, and the streams were lush with watercress. I was in the front seat, looking at the scenery and chatting amiably with Mr. Twining, whom I was beginning to think of as Sam. Alas, his car was not a Daimler, but I hid my disappointment very maturely, I thought. Besides, I was captivated by Mr. Twining's conversation, which was laced with ex-

On average, popular blends of tea often contain teas from as many as fifteen different gardens from various countries, and sometimes more than that.

pressions such as "Jolly good!" He was speaking of his staff at the factory: "Ian is a very good man, with us for thirty-five years. Molly and her daughter have been here for twenty-five." His vocabulary and diction made me think of the exaggerated MGM stereotype of a mustachioed, upper-class, stiff-upper-lipped, standard-bearer of the Empire. But he had inherited this manner quite legitimately; and he was so genial that had he addressed me as "my good woman," I would not have been surprised; I would have guessed he meant it with all his heart, and I would have been delighted.

The inn where we had lunch was small, with dark wooden booths and a fireplace. We were brought lots of whole meal bread and a delicious fresh shrimp salad. I started on my agenda, beginning with my frustration at getting no response from his American representative about the Two Hundred Seventy-fifth Anniversary blend. Then he told me his story.

He himself had gone to China to explore the possibility of more tea. The Yunnan was dear to his heart, too. He had hired drivers and traveled all the way to remote gardens that supplied rare teas in the anniversary blend. He spoke in his best C.E.O. manner, calmly and quietly, but I detected the snows of his British reserve beginning to melt. He described meeting the workers in these gardens, how they had grouped together around him, standing quietly. His interpreter let them know who Mr. Twining was, and why he had come. (He leaned back in the dark booth against the old wood, and pushed his plate aside, setting aside more of his reserve at the same time. He was speaking in a different voice now.) He described how the workers had edged up close to him to finger his lapels, feel his hair, and stare at his shoes. He gestured to his lapels and his hair as he told the story. "I showed them photographs of tea being grown in other parts of China, and they were puzzled. 'Who are these foreigners?' they wanted to know. They were so isolated I had to explain that there were other provinces in China growing tea, producing different teas with different characters, where people dressed differently, and in fact were different!" Through the interpreter, they thanked him for coming so far to see them; Mr. Twining was the first Westerner they had ever seen.

He threw back his head. "Nothing, no honor or award I have ever received, has pleased me as much as that tribute." (This from a man who is allowed to write O.B.E. after his name, but never does.) He paused, reliving the moment. There was no doubting his sincerity.

"But what about the tea?" I pressed on. What *were* the chances of more Two Hundred Seventy-fifth Anniversary Yunnan? Alas, the tea gardens he had visited were "too much under the thumb of the Party." To get a steady supply of enough high-quality tea from Yunnan to supply "the Company" (as he always referred to Twinings) was simply impossible. "We shall have to wait for better times, that's all." His tone was like that of a kindly country doctor with very bad news who nevertheless has not lost all hope. His own acceptance of the situation made it easier for me.

It was time for dessert and tea. The hostess brought two ample pieces of seedcake, a stainless steel pot of tea, and cups. "Here we are!" she said, in a way somehow comforting and at the same time triumphant. To bring seedcake to an English gentleman is to be as sure of success as if you were to bring a plate of warm chocolate-chip cookies to a red-blooded American businessman. A real seedcake in England is made with whole caraway seeds, and lots of them; this one looked solid, but with a tender crumb. I was right. Though usually served only at teatime, it was the perfect thing to have after a light lunch.

I commented on the teapot: Was it true that he preferred stainless steel pots? Yes, it was. They clean out so well, he explained, and if they are heavy enough they keep the tea warm without the bother of a cozy; he knew his view was unpopular, but he was partial to them, and as I must know, many tea rooms, hotels, and cafés used them, especially in London. Quite true, but to my mind they lack the warmth of porcelain or of dark, nubbly cast iron.

We nibbled our seedcake and gazed into the small fire on the grate. The lively, cozy fireside went well with the smell of the brewing tea and the spicy, earthy quality of the cake. Mr. Twining spoke of his delight in a fire after a long tramp in the countryside. "The fireside, some Lapsang Souchong, and perhaps a bit of seedcake. Ah, that's solid comfort for you." When our tea had steeped long enough, the official Mr. Twining poured solemnly. Then he lifted the lid of the pot and in a sparkling instant became Sam again. He winced, swung his head to

Lapsang Souchong is a black China tea from Fujian province. (Souchong is Chinese for a large-leaf tea.) A combination of factors—among them the soil and the climate, but especially the resin-rich pine chips traditionally used for firing the tea—gives Lapsang Souchong a uniquely strong, smoky flavor.

the side, and exclaimed, "Oh—bags!" They had had the nerve—or they had been careless enough—to make our tea with tea bags! We laughed, and took the tea without sending it back or making a fuss. And it was quite good. It was Twinings Traditional Blend, very much like English Breakfast. I had milk in mine. The bags were undoubtedly very fresh; and the water from the chalky Hampshires, which helped produce the gorgeous watercress, had enhanced the tea as well.

We headed out the door into the pale light of the courtyard. It was early afternoon now, overcast, and beginning to drizzle. It was an appropriately melancholy backdrop for the end of our lovely time together. I saw that Joseph had arrived with the other car and was waiting for me.

Mr. Twining turned to me. "Now, Mrs. Gustafson, you had some sort of carryall with you. Is that in the inn or in my car?"

"In the car, thank you."

He stepped over to his Ghia and opened the trunk. He pulled out my bag and handed it to Joseph, smiling and commenting on its heft. "Hmm, the family silver must be in here!" Then he became Mr. Twining of The Company again. He squared off opposite Joseph and gave him what was perhaps the standard send-off speech:

"Now, Joseph, do you think that you can safely carry Mrs. Gustafson to the station? It is not very important that I get back to my office on time, but it *is* very important that Mrs. Gustafson get to the station on time. Do you think you can ferry Mrs. G. past the lions and the tigers and the dragons and all those dreadful things, and safely escort her to the railway station? Do you think you can do that?"

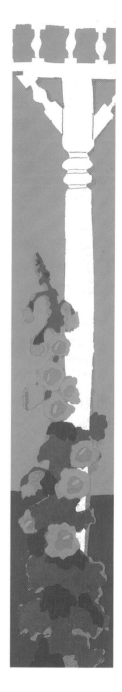

Joseph nodded solemnly, without the hint of a smile, twisted his cap in his hands, and said, "Yes, sir, I believe I can. Indeed I can, sir."

"Excellent, Joseph," said Mr. Twining.

Mr. Twining and I said another round of good-byes and thank yous, and as Joseph went to the front of the car, Mr. Twining handed me formally into it. We waved good-bye with small royal farewell gestures.

The car started down the driveway. A casual observer would have concluded that I was just a woman in a red sweater and a trench coat riding in the back of a little nondescript runabout. But the observer would have been mistaken: I was in a grand gleaming coach, drawn by matched horses, and attended by liveried footmen. I could feel the long ribbons of my eighteenth-century cloak around my neck. From up front I could hear the clippity-clop and the splashing of the horses' hooves on the roadway. We swayed along and I gazed out at the gray green landscape, fingering the mauve velvet upholstery. I snapped out of my reverie long enough to ask Joseph what kind of a man Mr. Twining was, really, and the answer was right out of the movies: "Oh, he's a fine man, he is. A gentleman. Good to all of us. My father and I have been with Mr. Twining, and his father before him, for over seventy years between the two of us. Oh, yes, Mr. Twining is a fine gentleman."

I sighed; yes, he *was* a fine gentleman. The expressions he used so freely had come to seem entirely natural to me in just a few hours. They were not off the MGM back lot; they were Mr. Twining's. He had been brought up on them; they *were* him.

I gently pulled my imaginary cape—and my tea world—around my shoulders. Trusty Joseph carefully minded the horses, and we proceeded with all deliberate dispatch, across the green fields and back to the railway station. Then back alone to London and the real world, and a few days later, back home.

RECIPES

English Gentleman's Sit-Down Seedcake

MAKES ONE 8- OR 10-INCH SEED CAKE (ABOUT 12 SERVINGS)

This recipe is a near twin to the seedcake I shared with Mr. Twining.

3 cups all-purpose flour	1 teaspoon vanilla
1 teaspoon salt	1 or 2 drops almond extract
½ teaspoon baking powder	1 or 2 drops lemon extract
½ teaspoon baking soda	1 cup buttermilk
½ pound butter, softened	2 tablespoons caraway seeds
2 cups sugar	(or poppy seeds)
4 eggs	

Preheat the oven to 350°F. Grease an 8- or 10-inch bundt pan. Be sure ingredients are at room temperature.

Place the flour, salt, baking powder, and baking soda in a large bowl. Sit down. Put the bowl in your lap, then stir and lift the flour mixture, letting it drop back into the bowl from a height of 4 or 5 inches. Do this for 3 minutes. Don't cheat; this hand-sifting is almost excruciatingly boring, but it is an effective way to ensure a light texture in a cake.

In another bowl, using an electric mixer on high speed, beat the softened butter and sugar together until fluffy and pale yellow. This will take about 5 minutes. At low speed, beat in the eggs, one at a time, beating for a moment or two after adding each one. Add the vanilla and the almond and lemon extracts, and stir thoroughly. (From this point, I mix the cake by hand, with a sturdy rubber spatula; but if you are wedded to it, keep using your electric mixer, set at low speed. Do not overbeat.)

Alternately add the flour mixture and the buttermilk, a little at a time, to the butter, sugar, and egg mixture, stirring just enough to incorporate each addition. (Overmixing now will cause the cake to fall when it is baked.) Gently fold in the caraway seeds. Tilt the bowl and give the batter about 10 quick lifting strokes with the spatula, like a kid whirling a banner. This incorporates some air into the batter just before baking.

Gently transfer the batter into the cake pan with a cup or a large soup ladle. Do this as if you were arranging prize-winning roses in a wreath for the Queen of Sweden. Smooth the top of the batter with your fingers or a spatula and place the cake in the center of the oven.

The cake should bake exactly 1 hour, but set the timer to check it after 50 minutes. It is done when the top has turned golden brown and split open, and a wooden skewer pierced into it comes out clean. Place the cake upside down on a rack to cool for 5 minutes or so. Then invert it and let it cool right side up, at least 30 minutes.

Some like to dust their seedcakes with confectioners' sugar; this is pretty, but not traditional. Seedcake will keep very well at room temperature if it is tightly wrapped in plastic. Stored properly it will still be good in 5 or 6 days.

Chapter Ten

ALL THE TEA IN CHINA

Home from England, settling back into my tea routines at Chez Panisse, I began to hear the buzz about green teas. I remembered what Alfred Peet had told me over lunch years before: "Black tea I know," he said. "That's chemistry. But green tea—that's physics." He jabbed his finger over his shoulder westward toward China and Japan, saluting another world.

When tea first arrived in England, all of it was green. What Samuel Johnson drank "in oceans" was green, and was made from leaves that had perhaps been infused two or three times. It was drunk from plain small cups holding no more than two to four ounces, with no handles.

After I had had my life changed by reading Norwood Pratt's *The Tea Lover's Treasury* in the early eighties, I had tried many times to like green tea. "It will come," Norwood told me. "It may take ten years, but it will come; if you're into tea, don't worry, it will. It happens to everybody." He was right. About three years ago he gave me a tiny packet of a green tea, an expensive Imperial Pluck, and in a lonely, quiet moment I brewed it correctly. As its super smoothness and delicate flavor lingered on my tongue, I realized that my mood had changed

Oolong—*bohea
(pronounced bo-
HEE)—and China green
teas predominated in
England until the 1850s.
The first Indian black teas
were not immediately liked
and were described as
"burnt" teas. To this day,
waitresses in England may
greet your tea order with
"China or India?"*

When hot, the small
handleless teacups
*of the eighteenth century had
to be held by pinching the
top and the bottom of the
cup between thumb and
forefinger. The remaining
fingers fan out, pointing
skyward. I think the prissy
lifted-pinkie gesture came
from this habit.*

> Fine Plucking" is "two leaves and a bud." The choicest of the choice, however, is the
> one little central bud with no flanking leaves, which is called the Imperial Pluck.
> Such teas can cost hundreds, even thousands of dollars a pound. Inferior teas are
> harvested by machine from the leaves growing much farther down the branches and end
> up in tea bags.

---

from a rather thin loneliness to a relaxed, powerful peacefulness. I phoned him up to announce my conversion. The tea, Eshan Pekoe, has become my favorite green tea. Norwood loves it so, I believe it runs in his veins.

Just a year or two ago, like a fresh breeze from the ocean, many more green teas swept into the Bay Area. And as trade expanded with China, *white* teas—teas that most tea professionals here had only heard of and dreamt about—were suddenly available for the first time ever. In the mail one day came an invitation to a once-in-a-lifetime tea-tasting event to be hosted by Roy Fong, the owner of the Imperial Tea Court in San Francisco, and orchestrated by tea buyer David Hoffman. We were to taste the hundred best green and white teas selected by the Chinese government trade board, and spend six exhilarating, heady Mondays doing so. The Tea Court is the only authentic Chinese tea room in the Western Hemisphere.

Holding the invitation I felt for a moment like the Southern belle who says, "Not for all the tea in China, Mister Ballard, would I marry you. I am *far* too busy." I was busy, it was true. But a second look at the invitation—rare green and white teas, the hundred best teas in China!—and I knew I had to go. And everyone would be there.

Getting to the first tasting was even more difficult than those trips to the Waters Upton Tea Room. It was a rainy afternoon, the streets of San Francisco were clogged with a thousand more cars than usual, and major arteries were blocked for yet another Forty-Niners' victory parade. Thoroughly annoyed by the delays, I wondered why on earth all these 'Niner fans weren't back home having victory tea parties instead.

The Imperial Tea Court in San Francisco's Chinatown is a heavenly place. The peaceful atmosphere created by its dark rosewood tables and moss green silk-paneled walls lets you settle in. And what a relief after the ordeal of getting there.

Everyone *was* there: tea brokers from southern California, a tea buyer from Seattle who specializes in organic teas, a sommelier from a famous San Francisco restaurant whose sideline is fine tea, and a journalist or two—plus the local tea mafia: Norwood Pratt, my mentor and guide; Darrell Corti, an expert purveyor of fine foods and wines who has now focused his expertise on green teas; Roy and Grace Fong, our hosts; David Hoffman, the mastermind of the affair; Mike Spillane, a West Coast tea broker; Lynn Frydryk, proprietor of an East Bay tea-and-coffee shop; and Paul Katzeff, owner of a similar shop in Mendocino. It was exciting to be in a room with so many tea people, especially as Roy is the only practicing tea master in this part of the world.

We were all keyed up and somewhat tentative, sort of edging around the room, unsure of the protocol; but when David Hoffman set up all the tea paraphernalia we were drawn toward the long central table like iron filings to a magnet. David's pace was careful and calm as he placed in the center of the table the large tea plate for catching drips, the ranks of tiny drinking cups, and finally the small covered brewing vessel, the *zhong* (pronounced chung). Nearby were low rectangular boxes holding small

To make green tea in a simple way (and correctly, without a thermometer), use a small saucepan and bottled spring water or filtered water. Watch carefully as it heats and when tiny bubbles appear on the bottom of the pan pour immediately over the tea leaves in the prepared pot. The water will be about 160° to 180°F, perfect for green tea.

Green and white teas, unlike black teas, never undergo fermentation. All chemical change in the leaf is arrested by heat, either by firing or steaming the leaf within six to eight hours of the time it is picked.

Roy Fong's favorite tea, the exquisite Ti Kuan Yin, originated in the high Wuyi country, an area so high and craggy that monkeys are supposed to have been trained to pick the leaves. Hence its name, Monkey Picked. This oolong is purported to be a powerful anticholesterol tea and excellent for those with high blood pressure. Because of the way it is processed the leaves are not perfectly alike, and it was not included among the first one hundred, but Roy remains attached to it.

*If David is asked what his
favorite tea is, he pleads,
"Ask me an easy question!"
He says he has had Pu-erh,
the earthy Yunnan tea,
every morning for twenty
years, but that now he is
more passionate about
green teas.*

white envelopes in which the teas were waiting. After each infusion he poured the brewed tea into a small, three-ounce pitcher, and then poured us each a taste in our thimble-sized cups. Part of the skill of a tea server is the measured pace at which he can serve, while keeping up a running patter of description. David, graceful and centered, with perfect posture and long pigtail and richly colored silk shirt, was the consummate tea host that day.

One tea after another was poured. Soon the notebooks came out; we were all trying to keep our heads clear so as to be able to assess and describe and contribute to the group without being too dominating. Norwood, with well-bred Southern manners, moderated and translated for the less knowledgeable, keeping things moving smoothly. We were all deferring to one another, tiptoeing around in new territory. Not so new to David, Roy, and Norwood, but new to the rest of us.

Roy frequently left us to join a man in black who sat apart in a corner of the tea room facing away from the rest of us. He seemed somewhat folded in on himself and was quietly, reverently drinking tea. He and Roy appeared to be friends. The shadowy man, I called him. (He turned out to be a collector of extremely rare and expensive teas, which he stores in a specially built wall cabinet in his home. He has a proper square tea table there, and very rarely a guest will be invited to join him *if* he believes the guest appreciates green tea. Sometimes, when he can't drink all the teas he has bought, he sells them back to Roy.)

All the teas we were tasting were subtle—acute concentration required. About midafternoon, after a particularly articulate exchange between Darrell and Norwood, Paul Katzeff spoke up: "I don't know how to talk about these teas! I don't have the vocabulary!" There was a pause as we all sympathized. Then I said, "Don't worry! We're making it up right now!"

David's smile was sparkling as he said, "We're all in this together, and we're all learning together. This is exciting!" Suddenly we all felt collegial and the energy level rose. Norwood visibly relaxed. Roy, back from the table in the corner where he had been conferring with the shadowy man, pulled over a chair and leaned on the back of it. His low, well-modulated voice and soft round features calmed us all as he spoke eloquently of the teas we had been tasting. Then he apologized for his absences. "I have been learning much from my friend over there in the corner. He buys only the finest teas, and tastes with such discriminating attention, I have become a better tea master because of him." I was impressed. Only the finest professors acknowledge their debts of learning so gracefully.

I made a little covenant with myself: I will get behind these teas. I will get Chez Panisse to serve these teas. I will spread the word. I will bear witness! I will put a fire under Alice, I *will.* I kept my holy feeling to myself that afternoon, but I called her the next morning, striding around my kitchen, roaring into the phone. She reassured me, yes, yes, we would start to serve some of these teas, but progress would have to be "incremental." I was so excited I forgot what incremental meant. When I told her that I had seen the most voluble panelist, a man with an encyclopedic mind and an opinion about everything to do with food and drink, sitting there speechless, savoring the tea, his eyes wide and unfocused, gazing right out into space—the only time in over twenty years I have seen him like that—she understood. If this man needed time to think it all over, I needn't feel so bad about being at a loss.

The afternoon of the tasting Darrell and David set about developing categories and criteria that would make it easier to taste green teas comparatively. Roy and Norwood had long since formed a partnership, Roy naming Norwood honorary director of the tea room. Roy conferred with the shadowy man now and reported that the two of them were proposing an association to judge fine green teas imported to North America. We were all comfortable by now and began to enjoy ourselves, throwing adjectives and descriptions around more confidently. One tea was pungent, alfalfalike, vegetative, with a deep nose. Another was rich, mild, elegant, with a lingering sweetness and a liquor color of a pale avocado.

The names of the teas were relished and recited: Gallant Mask of Mirth, Down of the Damask Dove, Lair of the Green Dragon, Wistful Glen of Pewter Fog, Pirouette of the Dancing Cloud, Shy Panda, Lazy Water Lily, Evening Snow Diamonds. . . .

At one delightful high point, David slipped in a new tea, a little fresher than the rest. It was an assertive Dragon Well. Norwood was sitting next to me,

*Softly rapping one's
right-hand fingertips
on the table means "Thank-
you for an exceptional tea,"
or "Thanks for the service
perfectly timed." It should be
done quietly, while making
momentary eye contact with
the waiter.*

and as we finished our tiny cups our fingertips hit the table a millisecond apart. Then he stamped his feet and said in his broadest Southern accent, "Now, that's foot-stompin' good!" We all clapped and stomped our feet, and David beamed.

I suddenly wanted a camera to record the moment. "We should take a picture! It's like Paris in the twenties with Gertrude Stein and Picasso and Cézanne getting together and discovering a new way of looking at art! But this is happening right now! We must take a picture!"

"Cézanne died in 1906, Helen," said Norwood, chuckling. Someone held a camera ready. I became the director: "No, Norwood, you sit here, and David, you there, standing, and Roy and Mike, you guys are over here. Now try to look historic." Everyone tried.

As the tasting broke up, Norwood and I swung out through the tea room doorway into the purple twilight of a San Francisco evening. All the afternoon's events seemed to fit together, and once again I felt safe and secure. Reciting those tea names in my head had brought back the sun room again, the memories of grown-ups' small talk. And I began to roll my tongue over the names I had heard into those spirals of fun with Rutabaga. I could smell my Chinese doll with the stiff black hair and eyes that opened and closed; she was too magical, too queenly to be given a name. When I played with that doll I had imagined exotic music and paper lanterns at dusk. And here in Chinatown the world of my doll was coming to life in a new way. As Norwood and I walked past an herb and spice shop with lanterns rustling in front of it, I took a deep, satisfying breath. Life was taking a new turn. I felt young and eager at the thought of all the exploration and excitement ahead.

The energy of the tea tasting followed us as we strode on past the fortune cookie factory—a dim cavern of a room that opened right onto the street—and past the jumble of the greengrocers' and the shoppers' sharp voices ricocheting above the vegetables. We turned and twisted through the narrow streets, the cool breeze at our clothes and the fog starting to invade the passageways as we went. My purple jacket matched the sky. The jacket matched my outfit, too. One off note was struck by my sensible shoes; but I had added a dramatic scarf, a scarf not so different from what a faculty wife might have worn to show she

had some flair. I was enveloped in memories of the old Grove, so warm and genteel, where it seemed everyone had good manners and made the pursuit of knowledge paramount.

Tea has good manners, too, I thought. This fastidious plant will not grow where lightning has struck or man has built. I thought of the sociable way tea nurtures, never intruding, never causing uproar or discord. On the contrary, it remains benign, gentle, ever the enhancer. What good fortune, I reflected, to have had the luck (or the wit) to have had a teacup carry me on life's exciting ride.

At home, still glowing from the day's events, I slipped into bed without performing my routine ablutions, and went all the way back home to Minneapolis and my pretty red castle on the hill. I was fourteen again, lying in bed grinning at the glimmering possibilities ahead. The euphoria I had felt after the Faculty Follies Tea had been re-created in San Francisco. If we had had a banister, I would have slid right down it. Instead, I dug my toes into the comforter, pulled the blankets around my shoulders, and laughed out loud.

INDEX

9/96

IMPORTANT

Leave cards in pocket